Priest and partisan

Priest and partisan

A South African journey

by Michael Worsnip

OCEAN PRESS

Cover design by David Spratt
Front cover photo: Lars Pehrson
Back cover photo: *The Cape Times*

ISBN 1-875284-96-6

First printed 1996

Printed in Australia

Published by Ocean Press,
GPO Box 3279, Melbourne, Victoria 3001, Australia
Fax: (61-3) 9372 1765 Email: Ocean_Press@msn.com

Distributed in the United States by the Talman Company,
     131 Spring Street, New York, NY 10012, USA
Distributed in Canada by Marginal Distribution,
     277 George St. N., Unit 102, Peterborough, Ontario K9J 3G9, Canada
Distributed in Britain and Europe by Central Books,
     99 Wallis Road, London E9 5LN, Britain
Distributed in Australia by Astam Books,
     57-61 John Street, Leichhardt, NSW 2040, Australia
Distributed in Cuba and Latin America by Ocean Press,
     Apartado 686, C.P. 11300, Havana, Cuba
Distributed in Southern Africa by Phambili Agencies,
     PO Box 28680, Kensington Gardens, 2101, South Africa

CONTENTS

❧

To victims of apartheid

women and men

black and white

living and dead

heroes all

victors all.

❦

ACKNOWLEDGEMENTS

Thanks to:
Ocean Press for taking up the challenge of publishing a work of unclear genre such as this.
To President Mandela for generously providing the foreword.
To Archbishop Trevor Huddleston for encouragement and the introduction, and to the late President of the ANC, Oliver Tambo, for his words.
To Karl Niehaus for help and support.
To Michael Lapsley himself for sharing so much of himself with me down the years and for challenge and real friendship. To all the members of his family and his friends who have allowed me to use personal material in this book.
To the Society of the Sacred Mission for financial support.
To Ruth Lundie for, once again, producing an index for me. And to countless others who have helped me and encouraged me in the writing of this book.
For Brian for making the tea.

❧

Michael Worsnip is a prominent South African theologian. He fled South Africa as a war resister in 1979 and taught in Lesotho, where he joined the ANC and was ordained as an Anglican priest. In 1985, whilst working as General Secretary for the Christian Council of Lesotho, he was expelled from Lesotho for exposing the South African government's use of death squads to eliminate anti-apartheid activists. After returning to South Africa in 1986, he lectured in theology at the Federal Theological Seminary of Southern Africa. The authorities removed his passport for five years.

From 1992-95, Worsnip worked for a national HIV/AIDS education program. He is now director of the Association for Rural Advancement, a land rights organization based in Pietermaritzburg, Kwazulu-Natal Province. He is the author of several books, including *Between the two fires: The Anglican Church and Apartheid 1948-57*.

Preface
by O.R. Tambo

There are no adequate adjectives to describe the contents of this biographical sketch about the life and work of Father Michael Lapsley. This book does, however, come close to encapsulating the stature and vision of the man. It is the story of an honest, courageous and dedicated person, who waded through great pain and suffering in the pursuit of freedom and justice for the ordinary people of South Africa.

From the time he took his calling in South Africa as a young priest in the early 1970's, Michael embarked on the sacred path that all the really great missionaries have had to walk in South Africa: The path of scorn, scars, humiliation, but yet, the path of glory. It is a tale that is illuminating and edifying.

This book is about one person who cannot be claimed by one country alone, because to do so would reduce his international relevance. Father Mike, as he is popularly known, belongs to us all.

This book is fast paced, but it is also valuable as a history. And it is as human as it is piercing to the soul. This is not a book about Father Michael Lapsley alone, it is also the story of a people in pain, deprived and denigrated. It tells of a nation struggling to be born under the iron heel of oppression. This chronicle is like the smoothing of a spear — a task whose accomplishment is often hastened by the imminence of danger. Let us read it and draw from it inspiration. Believers and non-believers alike will definitely be moved by this short volume. I recommend it highly to everyone who cares about human dignity.

O.R. Tambo
Johannesburg
November 1992

Foreword
by Nelson Mandela

When I was approached to write a foreword to this biography, I agreed readily — even before having the chance to read a single page. I did so because of the very special person Father Michael Lapsley is.

This story constantly forces the reader to confront, through the intense personal suffering, the suffering of so many people in our country and the world beyond. Although historically located here in Southern Africa, it has a universal message about universal human suffering and our struggle for dignity and healing.

These are at the best of times not easy matters. But in the South Africa of 1996 as we begin the public hearings of the Truth and Reconciliation Commission, one cannot escape questions about how to approach those who have committed the most vile and terrible deeds, such as sending that parcel bomb to Michael. The Truth and Reconciliation Commission will help uncover the truth. But afterwards many of the perpetrators may be granted amnesty. Intellectually and politically one understands why this is necessary. But deep in your heart, and when you are alone with your memories, this is no easy matter.

Michael's life journey represents a compelling metaphor: We read about a foreigner who came to our country, and was transformed by what he saw of the injustices of apartheid. He could not remain aloof from the suffering of the people. In order to be true to himself, he had to participate in their struggle for liberation. What happened when the parcel bomb exploded in Michael's hands is vividly captured in the pages of this book. South Africans should be proud that we can now say: Never again!

The metaphor also involves Michael having been wounded outside our country, like so many of South Africa's sons and daughters. It can be further extended to his return and the many difficulties of his re-integrating into the society. This is a journey which not only Michael had to undertake. Many South Africans — young and old — had to do so when they returned from exile or prison, bringing with them the heavy burden of terrible experiences and deprivation.

A crucial part of Michael's own healing is the work that he is doing at the Trauma Center, where he is also drawing on his own experiences to help others. His suffering has become part of the healing, not only for himself, but also for many others.

Michael's life is part of the tapestry of the many long journeys and struggles of our people. In South Africa, suffering and healing are not a private matter. They are national matters, and that is why we need the Truth and Reconciliation Commission.

What Michael's journey tells us are truths which we have spoken and written about many a time. But they come to us loaded with renewed impact in the pages of this book. The most important message is that there is hope: hope for Michael, hope for South Africans, hope for humanity.

Nelson Mandela
President
Republic of South Africa
April 1996

Introduction
by Trevor Huddleston

Words by a former President of Zimbabwe, Canaan Banana, are quoted by Michael Worsnip in this book as "an apt summary of what is perhaps the starting point of Michael Lapsley's theology." I can think of no better introduction than to quote them myself:

> Neutrality at best means deafening silence and indifference, and at worst, smiling at and admiring the status quo. I refuse to accept that Jesus assumed the role of honored guest in the theater of human slaughter and misery. He intervened in human affairs and challenged the principalities and powers that denied God's children their right to life and to fundamental human liberties.

Canaan Banana's words were themselves an introduction to Michael Lapsley's work, *Neutrality or co-option?*, which began life as a Master's thesis at the University of Zimbabwe.

I have had the honor of knowing personally five of those who suffered for their commitment to the struggle against apartheid by massive injuries and, in one case, death. All were the victims of anonymous killers using bombs as their murder weapons. Two were Anglican priests and all were supporters of the African National Congress and its alliance partner, the South African Communist Party, as I am proud to be myself.

It is for this reason that I am glad to write this introduction to a book about Michael Lapsley — a book written with firsthand knowledge of its subject, but also with the passionate conviction that his theology is shaped and formed by action and experience, not by reading books. As I write these few and inadequate sentences, the violence which has engulfed South Africa during the past few years has claimed thousands of African lives and has mutilated thousands more in town and country alike. Even during the years since Nelson Mandela was released from prison, there has been no end to it.

Clearly, the struggle for liberation from institutionalized racism had to be fought within the country which has suffered such loss and devastation from apartheid itself. And no one can doubt that it is and always has been the indomitable will of the people that has provided the driving force for what is now a democratically governed free South Africa.

This, as I see it, is the background against which you will be reading this remarkable biographical journey of *Priest and partisan*. I would not dare to interpret it for you. You must read it, as I have done — every word of it, for yourself. It will compel you, I am sure, to recognise that in Michael Lapsley's life — and most of all, in the consequence of the failed attempt to destroy him by a parcel bomb — you are confronted with a personal choice yourself. Whether you are a Christian, a Muslim, a Jew, a Humanist or a Buddhist — whatever your ethnic or social or political situation may be — you are confronted with the consequence of condoning evil or challenging it head-on and accepting the consequences.

I write as a Christian, for that is what I am, and, as a Christian I entirely and absolutely endorse Michael Worsnip's interpretation of the significance of Michael Lapsley's mission.

+ Archbishop Trevor Huddleston CR[1]
January 1996

---

[1] Trevor Huddleston CR came to South Africa as a young priest in 1943 and immediately became involved in the struggle against apartheid. He was eventually recalled by his Community to England in 1955, but proceeded to publish his book *Naught for your comfort* which achieved worldwide circulation exposing the horror of apartheid. He became Bishop of Masasi in Tanzania and then Archbishop of the Indian Ocean. For many years he was President of the Anti-Apartheid Movement.

CHAPTER 1

"The Boers didn't win"

The telephone rang. I answered it. It was a mellow evening with not a great deal going for it. I can't remember what exactly I was doing, and in any case, who cares? Chris Langevelt on the phone.

"Mike Worsnip?"

"Yes," I said.

"I've got bad news."

"What?"

"I've just heard from Joey Lloyd in Cape Town. They heard it from London. Mike Lapsley has been blown up by a letter bomb."

"Oh my God!"

"What is it?" says Jane beside me.

"Oh Jesus!"

"*What is it?*" says Jane, desperate now.

I tell her. Her reaction is much the same as mine. There are tears and fear in her eyes. She wants to know. I don't know anything. Questions. I don't know anything. Chris doesn't know anything.

"Is he alive?"

"Yes, I think so."

There were a lot of telephone calls that night, Saturday, April 28, 1990. Michael's sister Irene[1] in Britain was woken up hearing the phone ringing in her husband's room. It was late to be phoning. Her husband put his arms around her when she came into the room.

"You'll have to be brave. There's been a bomb. Michael has been badly hurt, but he's still alive."

"What! Who told you?"

"Someone called Cedric Mayson."

"What did he say?"

---

[1] Irene Bick, diary, August 11, 1990. Irene kept a record of the events as she heard them and during the time which she spent in Zimbabwe assisting the staff of Parirenyatwa Hospital.

"He asked me to tell you. He had other calls to make. I took his number down. Here."

Unfortunately he had taken down the wrong number and when they tried it, they woke the wrong person who was very cross. After what seemed like a lifetime of trying to find the right number they eventually got back to Cedric.

Michael's mother had not yet been contacted. The New Zealand press and radio were putting a hold on the news release until she was informed. People phoned people, and friends phoned friends. The telephone lines were busy as people phoned others, often people they hardly knew or didn't know at all. The news was received much the same everywhere and by everyone. No one asked "Why?" We all knew why. We didn't understand *why now* — two days before the meeting between the African National Congress (ANC) and the apartheid government at Groote Schuur. Would it halt the talks? This thought must have arisen in one or two minds as they tried to grasp the whole thing , trying to fit it into some sort of context.

Nevertheless, the talks went ahead and the Groote Schuur Minute was duly signed. A member of the ANC delegation commented to me later that nothing would have stopped it. What did we expect? Perhaps some public statement might have been in order. I don't even know if there was such a thing, but if there was, it was certainly muted. Undoubtedly people had a great deal on their minds at the time.

Rebecca Garrett[2] and Hugh McCullum had just finished cleaning up after the party which they had organized to see Michael off to his new parish in Bulawayo. They were happy, feeling sleepy with after-party glow. While heating leftovers for dinner, they turned on the TV in time for the 8 o'clock news.

Suddenly someone is rattling the gate outside and yelling. What now? Hugh goes out. Rebecca catches the words "Andrew," "Michael," "ambulance," "taxi." The caller doesn't know how badly Michael is hurt. She is suddenly changing her clothes.

Andrew Mutizwa recalled:

> After the farewell party [Father and I] were in the house. Father Mike was talking to me. We were discussing about the house and seated opposite each other across the room.

[2] For this account, see Rebecca Garrett, untitled account of April 28, 1990, and May 5, 1990.

I sat on a single sofa and he sat on the other [two seater]....
There was mail on the left hand side of the sofa where he sat. I
was not expecting anything so I sat relaxed on the chair.
Father took a parcel and opened it.... I think I saw him take
out two books. The most visible one from the distance where
I was, was the one with the words "R.S.A." on it. It must have
been black or dark blue with the letters R.S.A. in either white
or grey. When he opened the parcel he indicated that he
wanted to phone Tito, who was booked at the Holiday Inn.
He got the cordless telephone from the library and came back
to sit down. He must have opened the book at the same time
he was trying to dial Tito because I heard a sound like that
produced when you dialed from the cordless phone, together
with the blast. There was a great sound and I thought it was
an electrical fault or something. I was not thinking of a bomb.
It was so confusing. Rubble was falling from the ceiling and
there was dust everywhere. I couldn't see. I got up and rushed
to the kitchen through the way from the lounge. The doors
were locked and windows burglar barred. I couldn't find [the]
key... [although] I had [them] in my pocket. I found keys on
the fridge finally and went through the kitchen door and out. I
thought there [would be]... more explosions, you see. I wasn't
sure. I went to the front. The gate was locked and I called for
help. I did not know that the keys were in my pocket. I finally
got them out and opened the gate. People had already started
to gather with some other comrades who rushed in to help.
We got in the house. I saw the shocking state... Father was
[in]. People were still afraid to come in as they also thought
another explosion might happen. Fire from burning papers
was put out and it occurred to me immediately that Father
needed to go to the hospital as soon as possible. A helper ran
across to phone at the Oasis [hotel] and I did not like to waste
time. So I just ran and got a cab to Hugh's house. I knew I
wanted transport to hospital.

I called out to Hugh. He opened the gate. We dashed in
and I phoned 99 to alert them...[3]

Rebecca and Hugh are in the car. A crowd gathers outside the house
in the darkness. Rebecca is running, hears someone say, "Don't go in

---

[3] Andrew Mutizwa, handwritten statement, April 28, 1990.

— there might be another bomb." But what about Michael? Where is he?

Sooty papers and rubble. Dim light inside. One or two people kneel beside a form lying on the floor, head propped against the wall. It must be Michael. She can't register what she sees. She can't tear her eyes away. She loves him and it is horrifying. He is horrifying but she loves him. Where did his hands go? She hears his voice, but what is that face?

There is no ambulance. We must take him to the hospital. Someone says, "No don't move him." But his torso looks OK — he's moving his legs and arms. He will die from loss of blood if we don't take him. Michael asks if the ambulance is here yet. No. We will take you.

There is no one to carry him. The policeman has told everyone not to go inside. Hugh is trying to find out about the ambulance from him. Rebecca finds them standing on the road far back from the house. The policeman is talking into his walkie talkie.

No sign of an ambulance. Is it coming? It's never going to come. We will take him then. No, you can't. We are going to take him. We will be responsible for what happens. Two more policemen arrive and help them get Michael into the car. Everything is taking so long. Time has slowed excruciatingly. Michael is asking for painkillers. He says the bomb was in a magazine from South Africa.

They arrive at the Avenues Clinic and everyone, except Michael and Rebecca, gets out of the car. They go to arrange for a stretcher. This seems to take forever. Rebecca is in the driver's seat and Michael is in the seat behind. She sees him struggling and says, "Don't move Michael — just stay there. They are coming with a stretcher soon. They'll be here soon." He is thrashing about, trying to get out, saying he needs painkillers. She reaches out her hand, wondering where to put it, saying, "Please, Michael, please just stay here, stay calm. They are coming any second." She touches him on the shoulder lightly to make the point, to restrain, to reassure him. But the touch is like a knife and he screams, "*Don't touch me!*"

Touch always meant so much to Michael — solidarity, comfort, encouragement. But now, just pain.

The stretcher arrives. Michael is wheeled away. Phyllis Naidoo and others arrive. They all hold on to each other. Will he live? There is a problem with the doctor at the Avenues Clinic. He must be transferred to Parirenyatwa. Jenny Hanekom finds a doctor and inspires everyone around with her optimism. Andrew returns to say that his ears are not permanently damaged.

Irene in Britain phones Parirenyatwa at about 11:30 p.m., and speaks to the theater sister who knows nothing about Michael. She phones around and eventually finds him in casualty. He is expected in theater at any time.

Michael stayed conscious until he was sedated for surgery.

"Pray with me Phyllis," he said.

"I don't know how," she said.

"Pray the Lord's prayer."

She battles to remember "... and deliver us from evil. Amen."

"Go on."

"That's where it ends."

"You *can't* stop there. You can't stop at 'evil'."

"For thine is the kingdom, the power and... the glory."

You can't stop at evil.

The bomb was a highly sophisticated one. It was placed in a magazine about the size of *Time*. Michael had received a letter posted in South Africa some time before he received the bomb on ANC letterhead from someone called "Mike" saying that he should expect some religious magazines in the post which he would find interesting. It read thus:

MIKE LEVUNO
2709 TAUKOBONG STR
ORLANDO EAST
SOWETO
RSA

DEAR FATHER LAPSLEY,

I HAVE BEEN REFERRED TO YOU BY "VUSI" WHOM I THINK YOU KNOW VERY WELL. HE TOLD ME THAT YOU WILL BE THE RIGHT MAN TO LIAISE WITH IN FUTURE WITH REGARD TO PROPAGANDA AGAINST APARTHEID.

I FORWARD THEN IMMEDIATELY TO YOU TWO BOOKS IN CONNECTION WITH THIS SUBJECT WHICH I BELIEVE YOU WILL BE ABLE TO USE IN YOUR ACTIVITIES.

PLEASE LET ME KNOW IF YOU WILL BE
INTERESTED IN FUTURE WITH REGARDS TO THE
AVAILABILITY OF PROPAGANDA INFORMATION
BECAUSE I DO HAVE DIRECT ACCESS TO THIS TYPE
OF INFORMATION AND MY OWN PRINTING
WORKS TO REPRINT IT FOR YOU.
THE STRUGGLE CONTINUES.

YOUR COMRADE,

MIKE

Michael received the bomb in an ordinary manila envelope con-
taining two magazines, one in Afrikaans and one in English, which
had been sent by registered post to a private post office box which he
shared with friends. Michael opened the English magazine ("I only
know how to swear in Afrikaans," Michael had often remarked) and
the action of opening the magazine triggered the powerful bomb.

It was, of course, designed to kill, not maim him. Had he been
sitting down at either a desk or the dining room table, the force of
the bomb would have hit him directly in the head or the heart and
killed him instantaneously. As it happened, he was in the process of
telephoning his friend and comrade, Tito Mboweni,[4] in Harare. The
bomb took out the ceiling of three rooms of the house and made a
huge hole in the floor. It splattered bits of Michael's flesh on the
walls and the doors. It was definitely meant to kill him.

Why did he open the package? Why wasn't he more careful? He
had just returned from a speaking tour of Canada and a visit to
Cuba, and was now on his way to a new parish. The truth is, when
faced with a pile of letters, human curiosity throws caution to the
wind. Besides, security was also much more relaxed at the time. The
government of Zimbabwe at one stage had been extremely worried
about Michael's safety. Two armed soldiers were stationed outside
the house. But then came the unbanning of the ANC and the release
of the political prisoners earlier that year. In this more relaxed
atmosphere the guards were withdrawn. However, what good would
armed guards have been against a single sealed manila envelope?

---

[4] Presently Minister of Labor in the South African Government of National
Unity.

Three friends stayed with Michael in hospital the whole night: Hugh McCullum, Phyllis Naidoo (herself a victim, along with John Osmers, of a parcel bomb in Lesotho) and Dick O'Riordan. Michael remained conscious and lucid throughout. He kept repeating his sisters' telephone numbers in London and Sydney. He spoke of the pain — he was given no painkillers because of the imminent operation. He wanted prayer. His hearing was badly affected. They thought perhaps he would lose it as well. His companions had to shout to make themselves understood. He could see nothing at all. They waited with him like this until after midnight; Michael in excruciating pain, friends not knowing how to help.

During this anxious night Rebecca Garrett waiting at home began to understand. She wondered at the amount of intelligence, creativity and care that must have gone into the making and sending of that bomb. She found herself getting so angry she could not see; but then she thought of the love, the hope and endurance of Michael and his friends and she started to comprehend... So this is the struggle.

Jenny Hanekom, a physiotherapist by profession and longtime friend of Michael, kicked into action. She insisted on finding a particular surgeon in whom she had absolute confidence, Dr Glen Gordon, an American, who, although on call and otherwise engaged came to the hospital immediately. His task was a terrible one — to try to save every scrap of flesh he could. Michael's finger bones had blown out leaving the flesh behind. This he saved in order to help in the reconstructive surgery he would need later on.

A long and terrible night for all who knew Michael. It had finally come. Michael was to recall some time later a remark made by Frank Chikane, one-time General Secretary of the South African Council of Churches (SACC). Chikane was himself a victim of torture, imprisonment and harassment. He had said that in a situation where there are victims and victimizers, if someone who is not a victim sides with the victims he or she can expect also to become a victim.

"I now understand what he meant," Michael remarked a few months later. "In my own body I have experienced suffering and crucifixion. But I am also beginning to experience a taste of the new life which one day will come to us all in Southern Africa. Today we must continue to struggle and sacrifice. God is with us and our cause is just."[5]

---

[5] Michael Lapsley, letter, September 23, 1990, Australia, and Hugh McCullum, "An attack that failed," in *One World*, May 1991, 9.

While Michael was in Roma, Lesotho, where he was warden to the Anglican Seminary students at what is now Lelapa la Jesu Seminary on the University Campus, many people would watch somewhat incredulously as he would look under his car for bombs before driving it.

Many of us thought this behavior to be faintly ridiculous, frankly. Yes, there was a certain amount of danger. That we all recognised. But that anyone would come and plant a bomb under his car, this, for some reason, we regarded as somewhat absurd. Perhaps it had something to do with Michael's own delight in drama and intrigue. Like many people of the same sort, Michael is an egotist. Not a bad thing, self-love. Suspiciously absent from many a would-be saint. There was a saying going around amongst the saint-watchers of the Church at the time. Let me tell it now. And let them blush for shame. The saying was that Michael was a little bit miffed about the fact that his colleague John Osmers had had his hand blown off, while nothing had happened to him. Could it be that the regime had overlooked him? If so, why? "He has a martyr complex." That's why he takes the public stand he does. I remember Michael saying to me in 1980 that he doubted he had ten years to live with the sort of profile he had then. I was chilled and I think I believed him. Truth to say, he imagined there would be a possibility of *dying* in the struggle, but he never thought about being permanently disabled.[6]

I saw Michael three days after the blast. I was not prepared for what I saw lying there. A blackened, charred face, recognizable only by the single gold filling in between his front teeth. Black charcoal flesh, burnt, holed, pocked, gouged and seeping. Two stumps heavily bandaged and trembling slightly.

Nowhere to touch him. Everywhere is red or black or sore. One tiny space on his arm which looks OK. His flesh is still burning hot to the touch. He holds the stumps up most of the time because contact with the blanket causes pain. He can see very little through his one remaining eye. We have to shout to make him hear.

"The Boers[7] are stupid," Michael remarked three days after the blast, "they have got it wrong again. They have taken away my hands, but I never really used my hands against them. I'm no good at

---

[6] McCullum, "An attack that failed," 9.

[7] Literally "farmers," but used to describe white Afrikaners and the apartheid regime.

shooting. I never was an MK[8] soldier. But I've still got my voice and that was always my weapon." [9]

"Whenever I have momentarily lapsed in my commitment to the struggle, the Boers have always done something either to me or to other people which ensured that I would regain my certainty about the justness of our struggle and galvanised me to further action.

"At last I understand," he said through those swollen, bleeding lips as we celebrated the Mass at his bedside, "something of the brokeness of the body, and the outpouring of blood. We who are members of the ANC say we uphold the Freedom Charter. Yes, but what we are fighting for is *people*. Just *people*. We are fighting for people to live in dignity and peace, free from the violation of apartheid; free from violence and hatred."

The one to whom we had come to minister, was ministering to us. I saw Christ there. Not in Michael... well yes, perhaps in Michael. Christ in pain. Christ with his hands blown off. Christ speaking to us through bleeding lips. Christ with one eye. Christ with a tooth missing from his mouth. Yes, I saw Christ lying there in that bed and I felt Christ minister to me. It was perhaps one of the most extraordinary spiritual experiences of my entire life. I saw not one single sign of bitterness or hatred. And that is God, is it not? I stood and could but watch and listen as this extraordinary distinctly Christian drama took the form of human flesh — scarred, burnt, dismembered human flesh in the form of a friend, pastor, fellow priest and comrade.[10]

Michael's hands were always important to him. In conversation he would lean over to touch your arm. His sermons and public speeches were as expressive in gesture as in word. He would roar with laughter and clap his hands in delight. A gentle pat or stroke of encouragement to those in pain and despair brought comfort and hope. And now he has no hands.[11]

A priest's hands are for ministering to people. With them the water of baptism is poured; the bread of the Eucharist is broken. Somehow in all the pain and all the confusion, Michael was able to lift his mutilated stump and make the sign of the cross — the sign of

---

[8] MK (*Umkhonto We Sizwe*) Spear of the Nation — armed wing of the ANC, otherwise known as the People's Army.

[9] See also McCullum, "An attack that failed," 9.

[10] Michael Worsnip, "Tribute to Fr. Michael Lapsley SSM," May 7, 1990.

[11] Adapted from McCullum, "An attack that failed."

God's forgiveness... and his?[12] In a speech delivered by Phyllis Naidoo some nine days after the bombing at a service for Michael in the Anglican Cathedral in Harare, she charged the apartheid state with the guilt of the crime.

> That bomb parceled for Fr Mike was put together by a pair of hands employed by and paid for by the apartheid state and supplied with the wherewithal from the state stores.
>
> When Abraham Tiro in Botswana and John Dube in Lusaka were parcel-bombed in 1974; when Fr John, Suks, Siphiwe, Wandile and myself were parcel-bombed in Maseru on July 5, 1979; when Joe Gqabi was murdered in Zimbabwe in 1981; when Mdu and 11 comrades were murdered in their sleep in Maputo in 1981; when Zola Nqini, 29 compatriots and 12 Basotho were massacred in Maseru on December 9, 1982; when Jeanette Schoon and her 3-year-old daughter were parcel-bombed in Angola on July 26, 1984; when Mike Hamlyn, Thami and 10 others were murdered in Botswana on June 14, 1985; when Joe and Jackie Quinn and Mary Mini were murdered in Maseru on December 20, 1985; when Moss and my son Sadhan were assassinated in Lusaka on April 15, 1989; when Father Michael Lapsley was parcel-bombed in Harare on April 28, 1990; is there any doubt as to who the perpetrator is?
>
> The single architect of all the above acts and more, nay much more, was and is the racist regime. On that score there is no doubt in my mind.[13]

Michael, too, was later to place the blame firmly at the door of the regime: "It was the South African government through its sinister Civil Cooperation Bureau (CCB) which mailed that bomb to me. The bomb was not supposed to injure me, but to kill me. Ultimately De Klerk holds responsibility for those covert death squads which nearly killed me and killed so many."[14]

---

[12] Adapted from The Rt Revd Godfrey Wilson, "A Priest's Hands," "Morning Comment," New Zealand National Radio, May 4, 1990.

[13] Phyllis Naidoo, "Speech delivered at the service for Michael Lapsley at the Anglican Cathedral, Harare," May 6, 1990.

[14] McCullum, "An attack that failed," 8

From his hospital bed, three days after the attack, Michael remarked somewhat triumphantly: "The Boers did not win, eh?"

The *Citizen* newspaper speculated, some days later, on the basis of "intelligence sources" that the attack might have been a "revenge attack" by the Pan Africanist Congress (PAC) following the elimination of a prominent PAC member, Sam Chand, and four members of his family in Botswana. The article alleged that there was "no evidence to link South African agents to the killing of Mr Chand and members of his family and only mild rhetoric suggesting that South African agents had possibly carried out the attack." The article went on to quote its source as saying that it was "most improbable" that it was the South African government because of the fact that talks with the ANC were imminent.[15] Michael immediately issued a statement refuting the charge, as did the PAC which, somewhat curiously, vowed to avenge the attack.[16]

Why was Michael the target of such hatred? Many of us must have wondered like Rebecca Garrett at the sheer brutality and inhumanity of the hands which put the bomb together, developed a plan, located an address, typed a letter on false letterhead to prepare Michael for the parcel, chose the magazines with care, inserted the device, and finally sealed the envelope and posted the bomb.

This person still has two hands — hands to caress children and loved ones; hands to clap in appreciation; hands to hold and to clasp; fingers to run through hair; fingers to type with and to write a note with; to potter about with in the garden over the weekend; to turn on the television set and adjust the volume; hands to cook with; to open a window; to file a letter; to pour a drink; but beyond everything... to touch and be touched with. This person or persons, as yet and possibly forever unknown, probably has a spouse and a family. He or she probably went home the night of mailing the bomb to settle down on the sofa and watch the evening news before supper after a regular day at the office — nothing out of the ordinary. When the news broke across the world that the bomb had reached its mark, was there a twinge of professional interest which passed over the twisted mind of the bomber, that Michael had survived? Because he shouldn't have survived.

---

[15] The *Citizen*, May 2, 1990, "PAC 'may be letter-bomb culprits'."
[16] *Zisa Factsheet*, May 8, 1990, Ref1.21.9.F 114 and *Natal Witness*, 3 May 1990, "Parcel Bomb: PAC rejects claims."

This person may never be found or brought to trial for the crime committed. He or she will probably die comfortably in bed and live to a ripe and unworried old age. This is the grand injustice of it all, but it is nothing new: talk to the survivors of the death camps in Germany; ask the families of the victims of the U.S. war against the people of Vietnam; ask the people of Palestine, El Salvador, Guatemala, Chile; speak to the millions of South African blacks who have lived with untold and never-to-be-told brutality all their lives; speak to the Mama who was smacked in the face by a white teenage thug in uniform; enquire of the "boy" who has suffered degradation and humiliation for decades at the hands of his white employers — relentless, perennial degradation which knew no end and which cannot ever be put to right. It comes as no surprise then, that Michael's bomber will probably never be charged, much less punished.

This is the tragedy of South Africa, a tragedy felt by everyone with the slightest hint of a conscience. What will happen to the criminals, the torturers, the vicious (but far from insane) murderers who, by their bloody deeds, kept apartheid alive and thriving for all these years? What will happen to them? In exile, there was talk about South Africa having its own Nuremberg. I remember this being discussed with passion and great feeling. The criminals must be brought to face the hideousness of their crimes.

What has happened? Have people suddenly forgotten what was done to them? Have the bruises suddenly vanished? Have the dead suddenly clambered from their graves and sung the Hallelujah Chorus? Is all forgiven? Is all forgotten? Is apartheid dead? Is the struggle for human dignity over and done with? Not in the least.

I have never heard Michael ask for the head of his attacker on a platter. But every decent person surely cannot ignore the attacks which have been so systematically made on the struggling people of our country down through the decades of apartheid and the centuries before. What is to be done? What can be done? Is all the hurt, the pain and the anguish to be swallowed up in this synthetic balm called "reconciliation"? How can there be reconciliation without justice? In Biblical terms, you cannot have *shalom* (peace) without *tsedaqah* (righteousness). There is nothing new or revolutionary in this idea. This isn't "Liberation Theology," but plain, ordinary, straightforward, commonsense. The question remains, will the Truth and Reconciliation Commission achieve a real sense of either?

Michael's healing was to be a slow and exceedingly painful process. He asked Phyllis Naidoo soon after the blast if his face looked terrible. She answered, "You look about as ugly as you always did." Only Phyllis could say something like that at such a time and pull it off. Michael has always had a certain vanity. Some find it galling, some charming. It depends whether one is in love with him or hates him — there are plenty of people in both categories.

Michael never was the kind of person one could ignore. When he entered a room, even before the bombing, he tended to dominate it, and people have always reacted to his forceful personality. To those who like him, he is witty (and he can be exceedingly witty), charming, larger than life, kind and very gentle. To those who don't, he is brash, brutally frank and intolerably partisan.

Michael certainly has the gift of the gab; he is a raconteur par excellence and can retell an ordinary event in such a way as to have his listeners crying with laughter, especially when among friends. On the other hand, his sermons and speeches, while not being literary masterpieces, grip his audience and shake them about by the throat. Some people don't like this — particularly people who are uncomfortable with his message. They don't like to feel foolish or that their positions are foolish, or that they are in some way involved in depravity and degradation or oppression. This counts right across the color board, as I have seen black middle-class people just as angry and agitated about Michael as many whites. Part of this is because Michael often pokes fun at people's weaknesses in a not too subtle way — always to their faces — and in a way that is not too easily forgotten.

The extraordinary thing, however, for those of us who saw him lying there in that hospital bed, was the complete lack of the negative elements in his personality. Naturally, he was sometimes highly agitated. He still worried about his appearance. Dear God, he looked terrible enough! His sister Irene responded differently, writing in her diary:

> My first sight of Michael leaves me somewhat relieved. His face is burnt, but bone structure seems in place even though an eye is gone. He knows me — can be touched on top of one

arm and kissed on one spot on forehead. Everywhere else burnt, broken, tender.[17]

Irene also recorded several occasions when Michael demanded a soft hair brush — he wanted to look his best, even in that state. Michael was almost immediately placed in the Military section of Parirenyatwa hospital, under military guard. His sister Helen had flown in from Australia to care for him and be with him, as well as take responsibility for overseeing his visitors. Helen, it needs to be said, is extraordinarily capable and forthright and she took charge of the situation immediately. She established a good working relationship with the guards and the hospital staff and in somewhat soldierly fashion herself, managed to stave off the hundreds of people who wanted to see Michael; deal with the hysteria and over cautiousness of the military; and be a friend/comforter/sister/fetcher/carrier/companion/psychologist and many other things to her brother who was at that time as dependent on the people around him as a new born infant.[18] He could do nothing for himself, except think, and sleep and talk slowly and painfully. Helen (and later Irene) was Michael's link with the world outside his pain.

A list of names was established in consultation with the Military of people who could visit Michael. Only a privileged few were allowed access, their names were on a list kept by the guards at the desk at the entrance to the ward; everyone was checked before being admitted, and needed to bring some form of identification which had to be left with the guards while the visit took place. The matron had decided on the night Michael had been admitted, that the normal ward was not secure enough and so set up an ICU in the Military Ward of the hospital.

The nursing staff took an immediate and personal protective interest over Michael, resisting any attempts to overtax him during the terribly sensitive period in which he was in their care. One of the nurses with tears in her eyes said to Helen, "This is a very good man. We must do all we can to protect him. He is a very good man." The care by the nursing staff and police bodyguards in Parirenyatwa was quite extraordinary. Reflecting on his experience of utter dependence, Michael later commented, "I was very struck by the

---

[17] Bick, diary.
[18] Michael Lapsley, letter, September 23, 1990, Australia.

way the nurses treated me with respect. It would have been easy for them to treat me just as flesh, as an object."[19]

Instead they went way beyond the bounds of their duties and became so involved with Michael that they were often part of the communion services which were held around his bedside. Michael was to write a year later: "I have the highest praise for the quality of medical care and concern for my security shown by all the medical staff at Parirenyatwa, by the cleaners, the soldiers, the kitchen staff, the police, the nurses, the doctors... I thank you for your care, for your gentleness, for your love."[20]

When the time came for Helen to leave and for Irene to take over the reins, Irene wrote :

> She [Helen] is leaving this evening. She tells me of a bad 36 hours when Michael relived the bomb. Had screaming heeby jeebies and she had to sit up with him.
>
> Other people saved his life — I'm sure she saved his sanity. She is obviously exhausted. Has done marvels organizing Michael's affairs but he is now very dependent on her and they are both distressed at her leaving. I feel it's for the best as she needs a break and he needs to get over his dependence on her if he is to recover. I point out it will help his recovery more if she does go as he is now geared up to say goodbye.[21]

Irene's diary reveals a great deal about the sheer trauma of caring for Michael during that time. Before she left Britain, she found herself wondering about her own safety: "At some point [I] start[ed] thinking I mightn't be too safe myself if [South African] death squads try to finish Michael off. I think this through and know I could never look myself in the eye again if I didn't go. We're all going to die of something. I'd rather die helping Michael than staying home frightened and promptly being run down by a bus the next day. Imagine having all eternity to contemplate that folly!"[22]

It was the communion services around Michael's bedside, however, which were to have perhaps the most dramatic impact on

---

[19] D. Sinclair, "Finding God in an evil act," *Observer*, 18

[20] Michael Lapsley, Reflections at the Mass of Thanksgiving, April 27, 1991, Anglican Cathedral, Harare.

[21] Bick, diary.

[22] Bick, diary.

the participants. Fr Dick O'Riordan had, in fact, tried to give Michael communion soon after the blast, but he was so badly burnt and swollen that it proved to be impossible and Dick just resolved to stay with him. A week after the blast, about 20 of Michael's friends gathered around his bedside to celebrate the Mass. It had been a bad night for Michael. A plaster cast had to be put over one of his arms, over the burns. At least one of the participants had their own personal difficulties about the ecumenical nature of the eucharist, even though it was to be celebrated by a Roman Catholic priest using the Roman Catholic Missal.

Michael asked to speak. His voice was surprisingly strong and he spoke at some length about the passage in John where Peter is warned of being bound and taken where he does not want to go (John 21:18). He spoke of how afraid he had been in life of physical pain, and yet, when it came, he somehow found the strength to endure it. He spoke of identifying with the Eastern image of Jesus, as being somewhat less than perfect, shown, for example, in one image as having one leg shorter than the other. He said that just because the Boers had got him didn't mean that he was very important. He didn't want to "flatter himself." He knew he had been on a death list. He asked people to continue to pray for him and reminded them that we are all promised peace and joy — "but not just yet." When the bombing took place, he explained, he had an extraordinary sense that God was being bombed as well. In a very peculiar way, he felt that God's promise to be with him to the end of the age had been kept.

The chief celebrant stood beside Michael and shared his stole with him. Everyone in the room participated in the prayer of consecration. At the conclusion of the service the small group sang the great song of liberation and freedom which, for most South Africans is the National Anthem, *Nkosi Sikelela iAfrika,* and Michael raised his poor bandaged stump of an arm in the power salute. Everyone wept.[23]

The symbol of the outpoured blood was to become increasingly real for Michael and for all those around him — not sanitized and prettied up as is normally the case in our churches, but the raw gut-wrenching horror of real blood, with a real blood smell and a caked blood look.

---

[23] Sinclair, "Finding God," 17, and letter, anonymous and untitled, May 6, 1990.

Suddenly Michael asked Irene for the cross which he was wearing at the time of the blast. It was given to him in Lesotho by his friends, Val and Brendon Hughes — a simple cross of horseshoe nails. Irene said she would look for it and went through his bedside locker in case it had been placed there. She found a stuffed plastic carrier bag at the back of the locker. She opened it and a sickening, appalling smell came out. She suddenly realized that it contained the clothes which Michael was wearing at the time of the blast, ripped and bloodstained, and forgotten for almost a fortnight. Quickly she shut it, telling Michael that she has found some of his things and would take them home to go through. Thankfully Michael had some other visitors with him, so he didn't pursue the matter. Irene told Eugenia Matthews (whose own husband had died of motor-neuron disease some years before) about the contents of the packet and they, not unlike two other women before them, who made the lonely journey to a new grave to anoint a dead body, made a pact that they would deal with the horrific contents of the plastic carrier bag together at Eugenia's house, where Irene would be that evening for dinner.

After the meal the two women faced the clothes; they were soaked in Michael's blood, burnt and torn to shreds. They were amazed that anyone wearing them could have survived. Meticulously they went through them, fighting back the bile, looking for Michael's lost cross. To this day, the cross has never been found. While it is possible that the cross he was wearing simply got lost, for Michael its absence became terribly significant. It was the cross he always wore; now the marks of the cross were to be permanently with him in another form.

Michael has always had women around him. Perhaps, to put it another way, women have always been drawn to Michael. A few have been hopelessly in love with him; many have indulged in that strangely satisfying phenomenon called the celibate romance. Many have rushed to mother him (with, I suspect, not terribly satisfying results, because Michael will seldom allow himself to be cajoled or coddled). Many have simply been his friends. It has always been extremely important to Michael to have a variety of friends, male and female, of different sorts and types and shades of opinion.

However, I think it might be fair to say that he relates more easily to men than he does to women. There is sometimes, I have heard it said from some women, a slight tendency to patronize. To some extent this is the common male malaise of our time; few of us men actually want to patronize women, but we do. We rely on women to tell us that we do and when we do, because often we cannot see it for ourselves. Some of the women around Michael have been bold enough to do so, but sadly not very many. In other instances, there is no hint of this male tendency and Michael is as direct and as upfront to women as he can be to men. In marital relationships he is always extremely careful to befriend both partners, even where this is difficult, and he has had remarkable success in doing so.

Women have always been there for Michael, and in his moment of extremis, it was women whom he needed around him — it was women who nursed him; it was women who flew across the world to carry his cross with him: women both extraordinary and ordinary. Women such as Phyllis Naidoo, Jenny Hanekom, Rebecca Garrett, Helen Lapsley, Irene Bick and Eugenia Matthews. The theological parallels are by no means obscure; in the gospels women faithfully follow the condemned Jesus along his path of suffering— to the absolute end. In many ways extraordinary, in many ways very ordinary, but they are there, and even the largely chauvinistic gospel writers don't try to erase their memory.

The special place which Michael has always held for Mary in his theology may well have stemmed from a slightly precious "Catholic" religious background, but it has not remained that. For Michael, Mary is the symbol of what the Church should be — the God-bearer, the *theotokos* — the perfect symbol of evangelism, a symbol of the Christian, in fact. A symbol of what we all should be; but more than this, he must now recognize more fully than he ever could have before, the diverse and powerful ministry which the various women in his life exercise, not only towards him, but to all. Michael had the overwhelming feeling, during his *via Dolorosa*, that Mary the mother of Jesus understood what he was going through.

Letters, telegrams and messages of support, anger and sorrow from around the world started pouring in to Harare — hundreds and hundreds of them. One, written in a large and awkward script from a fellow bomb victim read thus:

Dearest Michael,

The whole membership here is buzzing with love and affection for you; you are very precious to us all — those who pray are praying for you, those who express their beliefs in other ways are recounting with pride stories about you and what you have meant to the movement.

Viva Michael

from Albie (Sachs)[24]
Lusaka April 30, 1990

This was just one example, poignant because of the similarity between the two comrades. It would be impossible to even so much as give a sample of the range, the depth, the variety and feeling of the messages which Michael received. From archbishops[25] to catechists; from heads of state to ordinary citizens; from people with whom he had grown up, to people who had met him on only a single occasion; from religious people pledging prayer and atheists pledging solidarity; from ANC soldiers on death row inside South Africa; from Australia to Canada; from the Philippines to Zambia. The Palestine Liberation Organization wrote saying that if the Zimbabwean government presented it with a hospital bill, the organization would gladly settle it. The Cuban government, on no less than three occasions, offered free medical treatment for Michael. The New Zealand government was later to pay Michael's entire medical bill while he was in Australia, even though it had not been asked to do so. It is almost incredible, reading through the mountain of letters, telegrams, cards and messages that he received, to see how many people, and in how many ways, Michael's ministry and message have touched:

Dearest Michael,

What can I say
to erase the pain
your torture
and your suffering
to comfort you

---

[24] Albie Sachs is an eminent lawyer and high profile ANC member who survived a car bomb in Maputo, Mozambique with the loss of an arm. He is now a constitutional court judge.
[25] Among the many letters of sympathy Michael received after the bombing was one from the Archbishop of Canterbury, Robert Runcie.

to love you
and support you —
all these thousands of miles apart
you are with me.

Our daughter Tess spoke to her kindergarten classmates about you today. I wore my ANC women's shirt for you. I cried many times and tried to imagine what it would be like for you. I have a new job teaching English at Auckland Girl's Grammar school. You have been here to speak. The teachers have written a letter to you. They can never forget the man who came amongst them
so impassioned
so eloquent
so Christlike
but yet supporting armed struggle...

Your struggles will be new ones, but you are a very special person amongst people. I know you will triumph as only true fighters can!

My rosary beads came out for you last night my friend. First time in several years. They will be busy for the next little while.

Just let someone tell me that things are changing in South Africa.

Those Bastards.

My heart is full of HATE for those who did this to you and for this I apologize to no one.

I am thankful for only one thing — that you are ALIVE! Can you remember how I used to say "take care?" I knew you would be a target. And you just used to smile — a wry little smile that you have.

I told you of my fears and you would mumble something. I thought of you, often praying that you would be kept from the inevitable.

After I had finished speaking to one of my classes about you, one of my very quiet students — Catherine — came up to me and told me that her best friend's uncle was John Osmers. The tears were in my eyes again.

Today you are in the thoughts of thousands and in the souls of millions. And you are very much in mine.

I can't say "Please take care," but I can say
KIA KAHA
KIA KAHA
KIA KAHA

My love

Kitch [26]

Another letter from a student at the University of Alberta, Canada, is also interesting because it demonstrates so clearly the enormous and instantaneous impact which Michael has on his audience:

Father Lapsley,

You were a guest lecturer for my Religious Studies class at the University of Alberta this past March. I have it down in my notes that I was 15 minutes late for this class. I remember it was one of those days on which the option to go back to bed instead of going to school was very tempting and I also remember being glad that I made it to class to hear the last two thirds of your lecture.

The first notes I scribbled down after scurrying into the room, 15 minutes late, were: "1652... Gospel of dispossession... 17th, 18th, 19th Cent.."

Not very coherent, I know, but I had slept in. Other notes read: "S. African state violence is languaged as *Law and Order*. When blacks use violence, it is called *Violence and Terrorism.*"

After class I annotated this section in pencil with the banner "hypocrisy." Other notes I took down as you spoke: "1960 March 21, unarmed Africans killed — *Sharpeville Massacre*... Basic RIGHTS DENIED — land, wealth, dignity... apartheid state — Theology of Death. Goal of the ANC — democratic *non-racial rule*... "Sanctions hurt us, apartheid kills us!"

An annotation to my notes after class reads: "I now know a little more about S. Africa. How has this lecture changed my views? I am more of a democrat now." It was this week when I went to pick up an essay I had done for this course that I

---

[26] "Kitch," letter, May 12, 1990, Auckland, New Zealand.

found out about the atrocity another human being had committed against you.

I don't know what to say.

Thank you for your lecture, for sharing your firsthand experience with us. The reports that we read in our newspapers seem so distant, and so incomplete. Your lecture to our class that day has had an impact.

Have strength, sir, let it grow, let your strength grow.

May justice — TRUE justice — prevail.

Once again, thank you for your lecture.

Sincerely

Jason Hoy
Edmonton, Alberta,
Canada[27]

Not all the letters he received were of a serious tone. Caroline Brown from Calvary, Canada, had seen a photo of Michael wearing his battered tweed jacket, the same one he had worn seven years previously on another trip to the city. "I hope," she asked wryly, "the bastards didn't get the jacket." "No," Michael wrote back gleefully, "they didn't!"[28]

I remember buying that tweed jacket with Michael in Manchester, Britain, in 1983; we found it on a sale and both bought identical jackets. Mine has since been confined to the annals of history. Michael's, evidently, soldiers on. I can see Michael taking a great delight in it though, the older and more worn it became. Not that Michael is a "povertician," like so many Religious. He is not in any way romantic about poverty. Michael delights in good things. Especially, it needs to be said, electronic things! He had, I believe, an enormous television set in Harare, a rather rare commodity in the Zimbabwe of the time. A somewhat socialistically puritanical friend happened to visit him and could not help but notice the television set. "You see," said Michael impishly, "that's what socialism is all about! It means we can all have television sets like this!"

---

[27] J. Hoy, letter, Alberta, Canada, May 3, 1990.
[28] Sinclair, "Finding God," 18

Although Michael has extremely firm beliefs, he has no time whatsoever for scrupulosity. He used to tell a story to his students at Lelapa la Jesu to illustrate scrupulosity:

A priest was called out after midnight to administer the Holy Eucharist to a dying parishoner. However, it was late and the priest was somewhat clumsy and he dropped the host in amongst the bed-clothes. He couldn't find it and eventually succeeded in crushing it to bits. In scrupulous zeal, the priest demanded that the dying patient should be lifted up and the sheets removed from under him. These he then took home with him, to be disposed of in a scrupulously correct manner. It was, however, as I have said, very late, and so the priest decided to put the sheets in the tabernacle, where the reserved sacrament is usually kept, in order to deal with it at a more respectable hour. What he forgot was that another priest would be taking Mass in a couple of hours and would have to contend with yards and yards of hospital bedsheets which had now somehow become part of the body of Christ!

Michael always encouraged care, both in church and in politics — but he despises mindless scrupulosity and Pharisaism of any kind. In this spirit, it delighted Michael enormously when his surgeon, Dr Gordon, who was becoming worried about his lack of appetite, suggested to Irene that she give him anything he wanted, including whiskey. The idea of a Methodist surgeon prescribing alcohol appealed enormously to Michael.[29] The military authorities were extremely upset about it, however, not only because it was alcohol, but because of the still existent danger of someone trying to finish Michael off: something could be hidden in bunches of flowers; fruit could be poisoned; all Michael's mail had to be screened before being taken in to him and no flowers were ever allowed. The military authorities finally agreed that Michael could keep his whiskey, provided it was kept out of sight in his locker. This was, Irene felt, a "reasonable compromise." However, shortly afterwards, his drugs were changed and alcohol forbidden, so the whiskey was soon stopped for other reasons.

Perhaps the worst aspect of the military clampdown was the restriction on visitors. As Michael's health began to improve, he naturally desired to see more and more people. Nonetheless, the military insisted on a reduction of visitors for the sake of Michael's safety — and that, hard though it was, everyone could accept.

---

[29] Bick, diary.

So slowly, agonizingly, Michael began to improve; bathing exhausted him, X-rays were a major trauma — but slowly he improved. Just two months after the bombing, with assistance he wrote:

Dear Friend,

On Saturday evening, April 28, I opened a letter bomb which had been sent from South Africa to kill me. I am alive! My physical body is scarred — I had never been in danger of winning a beauty contest! My spirit at one level is as fragile as anyone in the human community. And yet at another level my spirit is stronger, deeper, and more resolute than ever before in the commitment I share with the people of South Africa for a new and fully liberated South Africa, whose birth pangs are still proving to be so painful and so costly to so many. Hopefully and prayerfully, all that has happened to me will make me a more sensitive and compassionate person.

My personal road back to a full contribution to the struggle and more complete healing seems likely to be quite lengthy. I have wept and been overwhelmed and strengthened a thousand fold by the messages of love, of prayer, of support, and solidarity which have poured in from all over the globe. To say "thank you" seems such a trite and inadequate response in the face of what you have given me. One day I will try to tell the story as I remember it, of what happened on that fateful night and the story of some of the many people who saved my life.

Many of you will know that for some considerable time I have been a member of a number of families. Firstly, and obviously, there is my natural family. Then there is the Society of the Sacred Mission, the religious community of which I am a member. And then there is the wider family of the African National Congress of South Africa leading South Africa's liberation struggle, of which I have been a member for a number of years. For six and a half years, the Basotho people shared their lives with me. Since 1983, Zimbabwe and her people have been home to me in ways too numerous to mention. People from many other struggles and all corners of the globe continue to enrich my life. At my own personal moment of need all these different families have become as one, and so together we shall survive and we shall win.

As always — still in struggle, and with much love —

Michael Lapsley SSM[30]

Three months later, Michael was able to type a letter himself. In this letter he devotes some space to contemplating the extent of his injury and begins to theologize about the experience:

I have had to fight my way back from the total dependence of a new-born infant towards the level of independence and inter-dependence which is more characteristic of the majority of the human community. Until I am able to return to the struggle for liberation in South Africa, this is the context of my own personal struggle against the force for death which the evil system of apartheid embodies... God, and people from all over the world, have given me the faith and courage to fight back and endure... The kind of support which I have received has enabled me not to become filled with hatred and bitterness because of what has happened to me. That is not to say that I will not always grieve about what I have lost. Whilst I will permanently bear in my body the marks of disfigurement and disability, I do believe that I have gained through what I have experienced which will add new dimensions to what I can contribute as a priest and as a freedom fighter, particularly in the long task of helping to rebuild the lives and communities which have been shattered by apartheid.

If there was any way that I could "re-run the scene" and avoid the bombing, I would do so. At another level it has been a great privilege, albeit a painful one, to share so deeply in the pain and suffering of the people of Southern Africa.

In my own body I have experienced suffering and crucifixion, but I am also beginning to experience a taste of the new life which one day will come to us all in Southern Africa. Today we must continue to struggle and sacrifice. God is with us and our cause is just...

Sorry about the bad typing but at least I was able to type it myself.

---

[30] Michael Lapsley, letter, June 14, 1990, Australia.

[Then in his own writing]
with love in the struggle

Michael SSM[31]

It is impossible for another to capture the thoughts, the doubts, the fears, the major and minor triumphs which someone in Michael's position must have gone through along the path of healing and recovery. He would repeat to each fresh face which presented itself to him in the hospital ward, the catalog of his disfigurements: "I have lost both my hands and an eye. I have very little hearing."

It was almost (or so it seemed to me) that he was telling this to himself, over and over again — so that there could be no illusions about the extent of his injury. He sometimes would re-live the bomb at night — and the experience would leave him emotionally battered and physically weakened. After his first bath he was horrified to see his hands — or lack of them.

Irene tells in her diary of a brightly colored flower which her child Elizabeth drew for Michael and which she showed him on her arrival in Harare. He could see the flower and distinguish the colors. Together with the flower, a large banner which had been placed around the pulpit in Harare Cathedral for the service of prayer for Michael was taped on the wall. As the weeks went by, other children drew other flowers and these too were taped on the walls where he could see them. In fact, Michael became desperate to see children and, even though children under 12 were not allowed in the ward, Jenny Hanekom organized for her two boys to come and see him — together with pictures to go up beside Elizabeth's flower. Eugenia Matthews' children, Tendai and Michael's godson, Tigere, were present at one of the Masses celebrated at Michael's bedside.

As it happened, everyone's worst fears were not realized: Michael could hear — not perfectly, but he could hear — and see through his remaining eye. And his tongue was left entirely intact: "The Boers didn't win — eh?"

---

[31] Michael Lapsley, letter, September 23, 1990, Australia. In May, David Wells flew with Michael to Australia for a further six months' medical treatment. His sister Helen and her husband Clive Hale provided crucial support during this time.

❦CHAPTER 2

The violence of the gospel

There are a few (I suppose there must be) who would say that Michael deserved it. I can hear them now: what was a priest doing, going around the world urging sanctions against Pretoria? The ANC is a terrorist organization and he had no business belonging to it — not only that, but he isn't even a South African.

Michael was born in Hastings, New Zealand on June 2, 1949 — at the very beginning of the apartheid era in South Africa. His family background was remarkably ordinary. His parents were very devout Christians and baptized the fifth of their seven children, "Alan Michael." When Michael entered the Society of the Sacred Mission (SSM)[1] at the tender age of seventeen, he dropped the name "Alan" and took his second name as his religious name.

His first contact with South Africa happened some years before his entering the religious life when, at the age of thirteen, he read Trevor Huddleston's *Naught for your comfort*, which made "an indelible impression" on Michael.[2] Both Huddleston's book and Huddleston the man have had a tremendous influence on him ever since. In moments of crisis, it has often been Huddleston's advice which Michael has sought out. It was certainly the book which opened the eyes of this young, impressionable New Zealand boy, to some of the realities of apartheid South Africa. After reading *Naught for your comfort*, Michael felt "that apartheid was evil and the opposite of Christianity... I was angered by what white people were doing to black people. I understood Christianity to be about love and justice for all, whereas apartheid seemed like death and misery for the majority in South Africa."[3]

---

[1] SSM is a Religious Order in the Anglican or Episcopal Church.
[2] Michael Lapsley, "Why I joined the African National Congress — The option for life," *PCR Information*, Geneva, 1983, 63.
[3] Lapsley, "Why I joined the ANC," 63.

Years later, Michael was to repeat again and again the powerful impact that Huddleston's book had on him. "As a child in New Zealand," he recalled, "I read about apartheid in South Africa and was horrified by what I read. Trevor Huddleston's... [book] shocked me with its accounts of police brutality and forced removal of black people because they lived in the "wrong" area. What worried me was the claim that the perpetrators of apartheid were Christian."[4]

Michael arrived in South Africa in 1973 at the age of 24 and enrolled at the University of Natal (Durban) where he also worked as a chaplain to students on two black campuses and one white campus until 1976. Doubtless, he admits, he arrived in South Africa somewhat starry-eyed and naive. His theological and philosophical background and training had not equipped him for what he was to find here.

> Before I went to South Africa, I thought of myself as a human being. On arrival in South Africa, my humanness was removed and I became a white man. There was nothing I could do to escape from my whiteness. It defined every aspect of my own existence — the suburb I lived in; the beach where I could swim; the entrance to the post office that I could use; the toilet I could enter and so on *ad infinitum*. I could say verbally that I was opposed to apartheid, that I believed that all people were equal. It made no difference what I said. I was white and had all the advantages of being white. Whiteness became to me like leprosy. I couldn't escape from it. It wouldn't wash off. It may sound naive, but I didn't understand until I lived in South Africa that the system divided everyone into oppressed or oppressors and that structurally speaking, I myself had become an oppressor.[5]

Further, he reflected:

> More and more, the South African experience forced me to rethink everything I had ever believed about peace, love, justice, freedom, violence and nonviolence and the supposed

---

[4] Michael Lapsley, "The struggle is also my life," 1987, 1.
[5] Lapsley, "The struggle is also my life."

neutrality of the Christian gospel. I can no longer read the Bible and find the same words I used to find.[6]

At the National Conference of the Anglican Students' Federation (ASF) of 1976, Michael was chosen to be National Chaplain. This portfolio meant that he was expected to visit all the campuses on which there were Anglican Societies (ANSOCS) to pastor the students and resident chaplains and to liaise with the bishops where necessary. The job brought Michael into very close working contact with students throughout the country from very different racial backgrounds. It was this close contact which perhaps gave Michael a view of the situation which few other white clergy would have had.

Throughout his writing and interviews, Michael recalls this experience: "I am told by the psychologists that the most formative years of a person's life are the first seven years. That may be so, but for me the years 1973-76, spent as a university Chaplain in South Africa, transformed me more radically than any previous experience."[7]

Michael came to South Africa a committed pacifist. So convinced, in fact, that he felt his own father had been wrong to participate in the war against Hitler.[8] At school, Michael refused to march with the rest in army drill, which was something unheard of. He was summoned to appear before the powers that be, who tried to persuade him. He refused. The powers that be then said that he would be excused from this requirement, only with a letter from his parents. Again Michael refused; he would not ask his parents, because his father would never agree to such a thing, having fought in the war, after all. The powers that be struggled with this for a while, but Michael refused to budge. When they saw that it was impossible to move him on the issue, they reluctantly relented. He did not have to do army drill.

This story has a delightful end: Michael continued to pretend to his friends that he was doing army drill. What complex creatures we are and how great is peer group pressure!

---

[6] Michael Lapsley, "Christians and the armed struggle," 1980, 3, published in *Sechaba*, July 1980.

[7] Lapsley, "Christians and the armed struggle," 3.

[8] Lapsley, "The struggle is also my life," 2, and "Dietrich Bonhoeffer and the struggle for liberation in Southern Africa," paper delivered at the Fifth International Bonhoeffer Conference, Amsterdam, June 1988, 1.

"When I went to South Africa I was a pacifist," Michael recalls. "That is unusual for an Anglican priest, as there have been few wars in history which we Anglicans have been unprepared to bless. Personally, I believed that pacifism was both a tactic and a principle of the gospel. I believed that it worked in any and every situation."[9]

His speeches and sermons during the whole of his ministry in South Africa display a passionate and convinced commitment to pacifism, based primarily on his belief in the value of humanity and the human person. Doubtless, towards the end of his stay, the cracks began to show, but the commitment was still very clearly there. Even the day before his enforced departure from the country, he still argued strongly: "The Christian gospel makes it clear that every single person is of infinite value in the eyes of God and I do not have the right to kill another human being. I am convinced that our stance towards violence is one of the most important issues which we have to face at the present time. Failure to think through where we stand about violent action is a betrayal of our humanity."[10]

"Security in South Africa," he firmly believed, "is not in money or the gun — but in trust and love."[11]

> We arm ourselves more and more, but it will never work. We will never be secure unless we give all the people a share in economic wealth and political power. Is that suicide, subversion — or just the logical conclusion of the gospel? Even more seriously, all who live in this land have to believe in and act upon a common humanity which we share.[12]

He was convinced that people in South Africa did not communicate enough with each other. South Africa's groups of people either don't communicate at all, except at gun point, or they talk right past each other. We are a bit like disembodied spirits who go to embrace and pass through each other and both experience intense frustration.

[9] Ibid.

[10] Michael Lapsley, "The quest for a true humanity," speech delivered on the Durban Campus of the University of Natal, Feast of St Michael and All Angels, September 29, 1976.

[11] Michael Lapsley, "Hope after Soweto?" speech delivered to the University of the Witwatersrand, September 23, 1976.

[12] Michael Lapsley, "The Christian in society," speech delivered at the University of Stellenbosch, August 6, 1976, 3.

Michael used almost every opportunity to stress what he believed to be the authentic Christian option of "nonviolence." In his 1976 speech entitled "Violence and nonviolence and the Christian," Michael quotes Dom Helder Camera at length as articulating his own position:

> I respect those who feel obliged in conscience to opt for violence — not the all too easy violence of armchair guerrillas — but those who have proved their sincerity by the sacrifice of their life. In my opinion, the memory of Camillo Torres and of Che Guevara merits as much respect as that of Martin Luther King. I accuse the real authors of violence — all those who, whether on the right or the left, weaken justice and prevent peace. My personal vocation is that of a pilgrim of peace, following the example of Paul VI. Personally, I would prefer a thousand times to be killed than to kill. This personal position is based on the gospel. A whole life spent trying to understand and live the gospel has produced in me the profound conviction that if the gospel can (and should) be called revolutionary, it is in the sense that it demands the conversion of each of us. We haven't the right to enclose ourselves within our own egoism. We must open ourselves to the love of God and humanity. It is enough to turn to the beatitudes, the quintessence of the gospel message — to discover that the choice for Christians seems clear. We Christians are on the side of nonviolence, which is by no means a choice of weakness or passivity. Nonviolence means believing more passionately in the force of truth, justice and love, than in the force of wars, murder and hatred.[13]

But even as he spoke, events were taking place that were to change his views inexorably.

On June 16, 1976, schools in the black township of Soweto erupted in protest against forced instruction in Afrikaans. These demonstrations were violently suppressed. It is impossible to describe the feeling in the country after these events. Whites had the unmistakable look of fear on their faces: sometimes defiance, sometimes surrender, always uncertainty. They left in droves, falling over themselves in the scramble to sell up and leave. Finally *"It"* had

---

[13] Michael Lapsley, "Violence, nonviolence and the Christian," 1976.

come. As the smoke billowed into the skies of township after township, so the looks of uncertainty increased; the cocktail talk became more animated; the "solutions" more violent and desperate. Not that many whites would have actually seen anything untoward: perhaps the maid would have complained that it was difficult to get into work with talk of "tsotsis" who were "stirring up trouble" — stories honed to perfection to win employers on to their side with sympathy and some degree of leniency. Stories which would accord completely with the white employer view of the world, where the ANC was some external bogey full of communists and troublemakers and which did not include the maid — unless she was "cheeky."

On the other hand, blacks also looked different. They began to look whites in the eye. They began to say, very quietly: "Ja boertjie!" They began to look ever so slightly confident. They began to look as though the future was going to be different from the present.

For Michael, the events which were happening around him were to become a fundamental "turning point" in his life:

> Until then I had been a committed pacifist both as a matter of tactic and as a principle of the gospel of Jesus Christ. I believed that in each and every situation, social justice could eventually be achieved through nonviolent action. I believed that my father had been wrong to participate in the war against Hitler.
>
> There were several aspects of the Soweto uprising which shook my faith to its roots. All those who died were unarmed and were shot, in most cases in the back. The killers were part of a Bible-reading and Church-going people.
>
> In the South African context it is reasonable to assume that the killers themselves read the Bible and go to Church. I came to the conclusion that in the South African situation, for me to ask black people not to use the gun to help defend and liberate themselves, is to ask people to have a complicity in their own deaths.[14]

Even while still a pacifist, Michael had begun to understand the sharp realities and the implications of living in South Africa with a white skin.

---

[14] Lapsley, "Dietrich Bonhoeffer," 1f.

In the evening I often used to visit students at the black
Medical school. They had all the disadvantages of being black,
while I had all the advantages of being white. I was free to live
in 87% of the country, while there was only 13% of the land
reserved for these, who made up 80% of the population. As a
white foreigner, I would be eligible for citizenship and the
vote within five years — [citizenship] which is denied to all
blacks born in South Africa. I used to explain to black
students why it was better for them to use nonviolent tactics
to end apartheid. I also said that I rejected apartheid. They
used to ask me where I was going to sleep. The answer was —
in my white suburb. Pacifist I might be, but I gradually
became aware that the police and army would shoot to kill to
protect my interests as a white person.

I learnt of the four million people who have been forcibly
removed from their homes; of malnutrition; infant mortality
and even bubonic plague, which came not from lack of
resources, but the deliberate policies of a government which
[had the resources]... to house, feed, clothe all its citizens if it
wanted to do so. I came to see that structural and institutional
violence are not jargon but describe deliberate policies which
have brought death, dispossession and degradation to millions.

It was possible for me to say that I would not pull a
trigger, but it was not possible [for me] as a white person
living in South Africa to say that I was not involved in the
violence. Every day I enjoyed and benefited from the fruits of
violence in a system where pigmentation decided just how
valuable your life is and how long you are likely to live.[15]

These are themes which occur repeatedly in his writing. The shift
from pacifism to the acceptance of a position which acknowledged
the legitimacy, and even necessity in some circumstances, of
violence, was clearly extremely traumatic for Michael.

Even while still a pacifist, I came to recognize the degree to
which white South Africa and its supporters in the West use
language to shift attention away from its violence and the use
of state terrorism, so that the term "violence" is reserved for

---

[15] Lapsley, "The struggle is also my life," 2. See also Lapsley, "Why I joined the
African National Congress," 63.

the eventual response of the oppressed to the oppression and exploitation which is meted out to them as a daily diet. When a black person takes a gun to achieve rights which all civilized countries already enjoy, it is called violence and terrorism, whilst the preservation of the status quo is called the preservation of law and order.[16]

Quite clearly, the context of South Africa had begun to break down the walls of Michael's "carefully and passionately articulated gospel," which he began to see as "a set of words in sharp contrast to... [his] life of privilege... Delivered to black people, my gospel was designed to paralyse, and by implication, sanction the status quo in spite of all my protestations to the contrary."

Michael began to identify within himself a kind of schizophrenia. Ministering as he was to black students and being able to identify with them (albeit to a limited degree), but nonetheless living "as an oppressor" began to take its psychological toll. "My whiteness became a kind of leprosy that I couldn't wash off."[17]

He tells of a very interesting little cameo of life in South Africa, which for him was like a parable of the problem. Speaking in 1976, he recalled:

Just over a year ago, I was hitchhiking from Lesotho to Durban. Two very kind white people gave me a ride. When they stopped to eat along the way, I indicated that I would buy food. However, the driver insisted that he would pay for the poor "Father." As we sat eating I asked the driver about his work. He explained that he worked on the mines. Incidentally, he said that he used to beat the kaffirs. He was forced to stop doing this by the mine authorities.

Eventually he realized that they were right, as, after all, it had cost them a lot to bring the kaffirs from the homelands and train them. This man was kind, thoughtful and sensitive to me, but cold callous and inhuman to a person whose pigmentation was different.[18]

---

[16] Lapsley, "Dietrich Bonhoeffer" 2.
[17] Lapsley, "Why I joined the African National Congress," 63-64.
[18] Michael Lapsley, "Address to Christian students," University of Natal, 1976, 1f.

At the end of 1975, Michael had been away from South Africa for some time. Whilst away, he had read Nelson Mandela's *No easy walk to freedom*,[19] which was, at that time, banned in South Africa. He realized that he had unconsciously absorbed the white propaganda which portrayed Mandela as a ferocious "terrorist" leader who wanted (among other things) to massacre white school children. The book took Michael completely by surprise; he was deeply impressed by the breadth of vision, the depth of humanity and the sharp intellect of Mandela. He realized for the first time that what Mandela had to say encapsulated the hope and the political desire of the broad majority of black South Africans for a non-racial democracy in their country along the lines laid down by the *Freedom Charter*. Indeed, he read the *Freedom Charter* with fascination when it states: "We, the people of South Africa, declare for all our country and the world to know: that South Africa belongs to all who live in it, black and white, and that no government can justly claim authority unless it is based on the will of the people..."

How few whites have actually read this document? Many will, even now, comment upon the ideology of the ANC; make bold and ringing denunciations of its policies; or shake their heads contemptuously when Mandela appears on their televisions. But they will never have taken the trouble to sit down quietly and dispassionately to read for themselves what the primary and fundamental document of the ANC *actually* says.

The ANC has always been a fairly moderate, marginally Africanist movement; it strove for 50 years, from its formation in 1912, to bring about a more just social order in South Africa using nonviolent means. It was only after the shots at Sharpeville rang out in 1960, leaving 69 unarmed civilians dead and after the ANC itself was banned, that it reluctantly opted for armed struggle. This is not a history the majority of whites know, as generally they were untouched by the horror of Sharpeville in any real way. They were lulled by talk of a "biased overseas press, who took photographs of blacks relaxing in public parks during lunchtime and pretending they were dead bodies." Absurd, you cry? Not at all. Sharpeville was the fault of the protesters, not the police! Indeed and alas, Sharpeville's meagre 69 dead looks like a mere bagatelle next to the kind of figures we are used to today.

---

[19] Variously printed, but see IDAF, London, 1978.

In June 1976, the peaceful protests of school children were met with live bullets. By the end of that year the death toll had risen to over a thousand people, mainly school children. How does a convinced pacifist react to this kind of a situation? One unsuccessful attempted strategy was that of *Satyagraha*. Other clerical pacifists like Michael Scott had argued for this in the 1950's.[20] *Satyagraha* is the release of a kind of "soul force" which would produce in the enemy an unwillingness to go further and eventually through suffering and steadfastness, have desired effect. Something like it had worked in India, after all.

But when the bodies of a thousand and more school children lie side by side, many of them shot in the back, what in God's name does one say or do? What does one believe? "South Africa forced me to rethink everything I had ever believed about God, about Christianity and the world," Michael wrote in 1983.[21] He had considered these questions in an earlier article, "Christians and the armed struggle":

> While I preached nonviolence in South Africa, I enjoyed the fruits of violence. To be white in South Africa and to preach nonviolence is profoundly hypocritical. In the evenings I used to speak to black university students of how God requires us to be nonviolent and then drove home to my white suburb, protected by the whole battery of apartheid legislation, protected by institutional and structural violence, not least, protected by all that the Defense Budget implies. I would wish to seriously argue that to say you are white and nonviolent in South Africa can only be true in a very limited sense. If you are white, you are deeply involved in the violence, on the wrong side.
>
> South Africa explodes the myth of the possibility of neutrality for the Christian or indeed for anyone else. The very nature of apartheid means that there is no middle ground. The system decides whether you will enjoy the oppression of the oppressor, or the oppression of the oppressed.[22]

---

[20] See Michael Worsnip, *Between the two fires: The Anglican Church and apartheid 1948-1957*, Pietermaritzburg, University of Natal Press, 1991, 73ff.

[21] Lapsley, "Why I joined the African National Congress," 65.

[22] Lapsley, "Christians and the armed struggle," 3.

At the Natal Diocesan Synod of 1976, Michael moved a motion on conscientious objection. The original motion urged Christians to consider conscientious objection as an alternative to the use of violence to achieve or prevent change. The motion also expressed support for conscientious objectors. Legal advice made it immediately clear that to proceed with the original motion would constitute an offence under the Defense Act and section 2.1 of the Terrorism Act which allowed for a minimum sentence of five years, if the death penalty was not imposed.

In a speech on the Durban campus of the University of Natal in September 1976, Michael mused: "The irony is that if I suggest to black people that they shouldn't use violent methods to try to achieve change, I am acting as a loyal and responsible South African. When I suggest to white people that they shouldn't use violence to prevent change, I commit an act of terrorism!"[23]

The issue of the "just war" was becoming more and more important for Michael, as was the related theme of obedience to the state. As far as the latter was concerned, he took a fairly traditional line, arguing that "all Christians were bound to obey the state in all things lawful," which he interpreted to mean "that which is consistent with the law of God."

> Our understanding of the law of God needs to be informed by the whole canon of scripture, the evolving understanding of the Church and the exigencies of given situations in which we find ourselves today. In the light of... [this] I contest the view that Christians can ever, should ever, automatically acquiesce in any tenet the state makes upon us in matters as diverse as requiring permission to enter an African township, to the requirement that you should kill other people at the state's command.
>
> Personally I believe it is often a cop out for a Christian to say that s/he needs to do something because the state commands. [24]

---

[23] Lapsley, "The quest for a true humanity." See also Lapsley, "The struggle is also my life," 3, and "Priest must leave South Africa," *The Star*, September 24, 1976.

[24] Lapsley, "Violence, nonviolence and the Christian," 1.

He spoke to the students at the University of the Witwatersrand days before his visa expired, and he was clearly extremely angry. The address was titled, "Hope after Soweto":

> No, there is no hope for South Africa after Soweto, Guguletu, Mdantsane, Langa, Nyanga — the list is endless!
>
> Who caused the riots in Soweto? It was the communists of course. No it was the Tsotsis. Actually it was the ANC. Or maybe it was those meddling churchmen, Beyers Naude, Desmond Tutu, Manas Buthelezi, John Rees. Big Brother responds, "Law and Order will be restored at whatever cost."
>
> ... For several months, key black leaders spoke of the rising resentment against the use of Afrikaans by the school children of Soweto. I sat in the Students Union of Natal University in Durban and heard Dr Manas Buthelezi say that the children of Soweto have been on strike for three weeks. He said it. Others have said it. No one listened. How loudly did they have to shout? How many times did they have to repeat themselves?
>
> And then it happened. The first child was shot by a police bullet. For days it all just happened. And in a way it is still happening. The kill ratio was something like a hundred to one — one hundred black people to one white person. Like it always is. Your pigmentation problem makes your life one hundred times more valuable than someone else with their unchosen darker complexion....
>
> A new dynamic has been created in South Africa — by the children. Children who, in the past, were content either to die of malnutrition or accept an inferior education to prepare them to become nice "boys" and "girls," working for the white madams exhausted from endless games of bridge.
>
> You know, there is only one group of people in this world you can't con and that is children. Try explaining to a black child why they can't use the toilet in the main street. "But dear, you don't understand. Your bum is the wrong color." Who would have thought that the children would tip the scales?[25]

---

[25] Lapsley, "Hope after Soweto."

The speech was an emotional one. Nevertheless, it still demonstrates something of a rather touching naivete on Michael's part, as he continued:

> The gospel of Jesus Christ forces me (as only love can force me), to believe that the Prime Minister and his government are my brothers, for whom Christ died. Nevertheless, they continue to detain people under frightening legislation, among whom are people I love. They call people who tell things the way they are, agitators and communists, whether or not they fulfill that description. The labels are not important. The truth is. The things those in power have done to others, they can do to me. Of that I am afraid. But perfect love casts out fear.... For three years I have articulated a nonviolent position, embracing the values of peace, justice and love, as an expression of my commitment to Jesus Christ. For such views I am labelled a communist, an anarchist, and am told I am inciting violence. Friends of mine have been intimidated by the Special Branch because of their association with me. The Special Branch has gone so far as to threaten me in the street. Frighten me, they may. Stop the revolution [which] they and their supporters have made necessary, they cannot!
>
> I pray that I may be allowed to return to this land when all the people are electing those who will decide who may live in South Africa![26]

More and more, Michael began to see a similarity between the South African regime and the Nazis and consequently, questions relating to the idea of a "just war" began to surface. However, while he was still inside the country, these were only cracks appearing in his pacifist position. The more theoretical argumentation on whether or not violence could ever be justified was, however, far less significant to Michael than was the enduring impact of Soweto 1976. He recalled later: "For me, Soweto of 1976 was a turning point of my life. Until then I had been a committed pacifist, both as a matter of tactics and as a principle of the gospel of Jesus Christ. I believed that in each and every situation, social justice could eventually be achieved through nonviolent action."[27]

---

[26] Ibid.
[27] Lapsley, "Dietrich Bonhoeffer," 1.

Michael left South Africa on September 30, 1976, for Lesotho. Before doing so, he issued the following press statement:

> I am not surprised that the government has refused to reconsider its decision to ask me to leave South Africa. I regret that Mr Vorster has prevented me from taking South African citizenship and thus taking full responsibility for all my actions in South Africa. Although my imminent departure from South Africa is a source of personal anguish, it is nothing compared to the suffering of most black people in this country. I hope to return when there is non-racial majority rule in South Africa. I have always advocated a nonviolent position as an expression of my total commitment to the gospel of Jesus Christ.
>
> It appears that the government only approves criticism of the violence of the black people. However, the violence of black people is only a response to the structural and institutional violence of the apartheid system, which robs every black person of human dignity and at the same time incarcerates whites in bondage to guilt, fear and anxiety.
>
> The only relationship which the government appears to approve of between black and white people, is a master-servant relationship. Success in personal relationships across the color line brings the attention of the security police. Friends of mine have been intimidated by the S.B. because of their association with me. I have also been physically threatened by the Special Branch.[28]
>
> There is no hope in South Africa without the adoption by all who live in the country of the values of truth in justice and love. I believe that the Prime Minister should immediately call a National Convention, including imprisoned leaders, to work out a plan for a transfer of power to all the people. Failure to call a National Convention and white intransigence with regard to the sharing of power, privilege and wealth, makes support of the white power structure responsible for an escalating bloody revolution.
>
> With regard to my position as Anglican National Chaplain, I have been asked by Anglican students from most campuses in the country, including such diverse campuses as

---

[28] See "Threatened by police — priest," *The Star*, September 27, 1976.

the University of the North and the University of Pretoria, to continue as Anglican National Chaplain in exile and I now feel bound to accede to their request. I express my solidarity with all the people as they struggle for a free and just society.[29]

It is interesting to note that Michael appears to have already come to the conclusion, even before his departure from South Africa, that the principles supported by the ANC were "totally consistent with the gospel of Jesus Christ."[30] The shift towards the ANC position must indeed have been not entirely easy for him, not because of the ideological principles which the movement espoused, but because of the tactical option which it had taken for armed struggle.

It can surely never be an easy thing for a Christian to opt for violence, and it is a very strange kind of Christian who takes any delight in the killing of another human being, no matter who that person might be. It is always with astonishment that one hears of the bloodthirstiness of those who would reimpose hanging, for instance, where it has been abolished, or cling fast to it where it is still practised. Alas, so much of worldwide Christianity has been captured by right-wing and fascist forces, that all too often violence is condoned and applauded — even desired. The Church itself has a sordid history of blood, where instead of being the victim, it has become an ally to almighty oppression. Often the Church has served as the spiritual arm of imperialism and colonialism and the conquest of both has been through the spilling of blood. It was not unusual in South Africa, for instance, for the Church to condemn the violence of the oppressed, but bless the violence of the oppressor; or at least do little to stem that violence.

When Michael left South Africa for Lesotho, he did so as a public figure. He was emotionally exhausted and physically tired, but he was also breathing fire and brimstone against the apartheid government. He entered Lesotho something of a hero — certainly an example. The Anglican Students' Federation on ten of the country's campuses had asked him to continue as National Chaplain-in-Exile. This served not only as an enormous boost to Michael's confidence, but as an extraordinary compliment, given the times. The campuses included those as diverse as the University of the North, the University of Pretoria and Natal University's black medical school.

---

[29] Michael Lapsley, press statement, September 27, 1976.
[30] Lapsley, The struggle is also my life," 3.

In a tribute written to him by the students, it is clear that he made a tremendous impact on the students — one which they would not quickly forget. A white student wrote in the organization's magazine *Asfacts:*

> [Michael] has managed to establish Christian fellowship between the Christians of all the different race groups, especially in his monthly Bible Study and by his personal Ministry... Father Michael has exercised a necessary prophetic ministry to call us to repentance for selfishness and greed and it seems that it is for this that action has been taken against him. His expulsion is... a tragedy for the country [which]... has silenced so many of its leaders either by detention without trial or by expulsion. No sick patient can afford to ignore the doctor's diagnosis... and a country which persistently silences its prophets and critics is signing its own death warrant.[31]

A black student wrote in the same issue:

> ... you well deserve the title of "Brother, Friend and Pastor." We share with you in your uninvited pain. I am almost certain that not only will the ASF members mourn (yet in faith) but uphold you (as we shall continue to do) in prayer. Let us pray that Lesotho never becomes too far out of reach for us to see your compassionate face quite undaunted by the ravages of bitter reality.[32]

When Michael arrived in Lesotho he enrolled in the National University of Lesotho as a student. In those days (and this is still the case) white students at NUL were rare, so Michael was constantly being asked who he was and what he was doing there. Not unnaturally, he enjoyed the attention, but he also began to make very good contacts with various people in exile, many of whom were students. Among the many who influenced Michael, two people stand out particularly: one was Phyllis Naidoo, the other John Osmers. Auntie Phyll, as she is almost universally known, was a feature of Maseru life; fiery, dramatic, emotional, motherly, forthright and direct, literally hundreds of ANC exiles came to know her.

---

[31] J. Draper, "A tribute to Fr Michael Lapsley, SSM," in *Asfacts*, no.17, 1976, 5.
[32] L. Sihlali, "And another..." in ibid.

Her flat was open to all at any time of the day or night, and many made her home their own. She too had suffered when she and John Osmers had opened a parcel bomb which was sent to John in a regular mailing of ANC pamphlets. She almost lost her hearing and John lost a hand.

Phyllis, a non-Christian but with a Catholic upbringing, tells a story about John, an Anglican priest, which typifies the sort of person he is. When he came round in the intensive care section of the hospital to which he was taken, people tried to tell him the extent of his injuries. They told him he had lost his hand. He said that was OK, at least he had another hand. They told him it was his right hand. He said that was OK, because he was left handed. They told him that the bomb had taken away most of his genitals. He said that was OK, because he was a priest anyway.

It was to be Phyllis who would mother Michael in Lesotho and Harare years later when he was forced there by a decision of the Lesotho Church authorities and when he was subsequently bombed. How strangely intertwined these lives have been. Phyllis was to lose, not an arm, but a son in Zambia, while she was in Harare. His body was never returned to South Africa, although she still feels he is there. She still sees the things he would have seen had he returned; she still feels the pain and the heartache.

Michael and John are two priests who could not possibly be more different personalities: John is quiet, almost shy, somewhat vague and other-worldly, eminently likable, warm and loving. In general, people tend to react to Michael and John quite differently: somehow John did not seem to anger or challenge them as much. With Michael people either love him desperately, or hate him desperately; there is seldom any neutrality. Michael and John, however, have always been extremely close. They have both, in their various ways, been a thorn in the side of the collective Church leadership (despite the fact that John is now a bishop in Zambia).

Three years after Michael's arrival in Lesotho, John and Michael attacked the leadership of the Church of the Province of Southern Africa (CPSA) publicly over the position which the CPSA took on the issue of the Special Fund of the World Council of Churches Program to Combat Racism. The issue was an extremely volatile one for the Church, with Prime Minister Vorster breathing fire and swearing blood and destruction if a single cent of South African money went to Geneva. White Anglicans whipped themselves into a frenzy about "money for terrorists" and "communism," to the extent that the leadership of the Church decided to acquiesce mutely and withhold membership fees from the World Council of Churches, even though it was perfectly clear that the money from the Special Fund was not taken from membership fees and that it was purely for humanitarian aid in any case. Nevertheless, the CPSA was trapped in its own white dominated world, and hence immovable. The irony of the situation is that it might well have sent everything it had to the Special Fund, because from that moment onwards, white South Africa believed without a shadow of doubt that the Anglican Church gave money to terrorists and they withdrew in their thousands; or at least they stopped giving the pittance they previously gave and joined the reactionary Church of England in South Africa in disgust.

Michael and John wrote the following "Open Letter" to the Archbishop (then Bill Burnett) and the Bishops of the Province:

As two priests of the Church of the Province, we wish to make it known that the Program to Combat Racism of the WCC and the Special Fund have our wholehearted support.

We believe that the stand of the Church of the Province needs to be reconsidered in favor of a more tangible commitment to the struggle of the oppressed people of South Africa for a life of dignity and justice.

In the November issue of *Seek*, you, as Archbishop, are quoted as saying: "We did in 1970, and still do, however, reject the apparently unconditional support for, and identification of the Church with particular political movements or governments, for that matter. Such unconditional support is implicit in the manner in which it has been given to liberation movements in Southern Africa by the Program to Combat Racism and it makes the supporters of that program responsible for whatever such movements do which is inconsistent with Christian faith and ethic."

We have great difficulty accepting your statement that the CPSA rejects the "apparently unconditional support for, and identification of the Church with, particular political movements, or governments, for that matter." In spite of the actions of a small number of heroic individuals and some official statements from the hierarchy, the CPSA reflects in many respects, a Church in collusion with the system of apartheid and the government which promotes this evil ideology. Let us give you some examples:

The Anglican Church continues to license priests to serve as paid officers of the South African Defense Force, who are thereby bound by all the discipline and regulations of this army. When a Christian comes to the conclusion that the liberation movement is the only remaining vehicle for achieving basic human rights in the land of his/her birth, s/he finds that priests of the Anglican Church are in the uniform of the oppressor's army.

In cities and towns all over South Africa, in the so-called white suburbs where so many blacks work as domestic servants, there are Anglican Churches attended only by whites. Blacks have got the message that they are not welcome in such churches.

It is not unusual for white priests to be rectors of black parishes. How normal is it for black priests to be appointed to parishes attended mainly by whites?

It is easy for the far reaching expressions of racism in South Africa to blind us to the underlying economic realities which underpin apartheid. We notice that our Bishops choose their point of identification by living in the richer white suburbs of South Africa....

We are suggesting that by its actions, rather than its words, the CPSA has shown its lack of neutrality. Even if neutrality were possible, our understanding of the Old Testament and of the words and actions of Jesus is that God is not neutral; God takes sides and we who seek to follow Christ must take sides also. The Old and New Testaments reveal clearly the partiality of God towards the oppressed, simply because they are oppressed.

Our observation of the official participation of Anglican priests in the SADF makes it clear that, according to your criteria, the CPSA is responsible for whatever the Botha government does, verbal protests notwithstanding.

It appears that the World Council of Churches criteria that grants are to be used for humanitarian activities are not acceptable to you. Such unequivocal support for those seeking the liberation of the subcontinent you regard as unacceptable to Christians. You seem not to believe the WCC, either when it points out that the grants from the Special Fund do not imply unconditional support for the particular organizations which are attempting to combat racism or the means which they adopt.

If someone is white and living in South Africa, they have a privileged position which was won and is maintained by violence. The entire South African system exemplifies violence used by the minority against the majority. Historically, one Christian response to all forms of violence has been pacifism in varying forms. However, most Christians agree that sometimes the use of violence, in an already violent situation, can be the lesser evil, or even the concrete expression of love for one's neighbor. In the South African context, surely, the Christian gospel's demand to love the neighbor and its fundamental commitment to the liberation of the poor necessitates an acceptance of revolutionary violence by individual Christians as the only way left of achieving a more just society.

We note with alarm that in South Africa, it is white Christians who tell black Christians that it is unchristian for them to use violence to fight against the apartheid system in order to seek basic human rights; while retaining their position of dominance through legitimized violence...

The World Council of Churches has pointed out that the negative reaction to the grants of the Special Fund have come almost exclusively from Western Europe and the United States, while black African, Latin American and Asian responses, if they came at all, were mostly favorable. An economic analysis reveals that the major beneficiaries of apartheid are white South Africa, the United States and Western Europe. It is not surprising that it is people from among the greatest beneficiaries who have the most doubt about overthrowing this system of exploitation.

We recall that long before you were Archbishop, during the Second World War, you moved from a pacifist position to active participation in the overthrow of the forces of nazism in Europe. We are hoping and praying that you will make a similar move from your present position of attempted disengagement, to leading the Anglican Church courageously to a more tangible support for the forces of liberation against the neo-Nazis who rule South Africa today.

We realize that you are echoing the resolution of the 1970 Synod. However, we are doubtful [that] the political realities of South Africa make it possible for black South African Anglicans to publicly state a contrary viewpoint to the one expressed by the Provincial Synod in 1970. The Provincial Synod resolution notwithstanding, we know that your viewpoint does not express the views of many Anglicans who live in Mozambique, Namibia, Swaziland and Lesotho, as well as many black Anglicans who live in the Republic of South Africa — and even some white Anglicans. Are you not forgetting that in Namibia, for example, a very large percentage of Anglicans are SWAPO [South West African People's Organization] supporters; an organization which has been given humanitarian aid by the Program to Combat Racism?...

The hour is late for the Church in Southern Africa. We pray daily that you will offer the people a concrete model of identification with the oppressed people of Southern Africa — for the same of the poor man Jesus — who died to free us all.

Signed,

Fr John Osmers   Fr Michael Lapsley SSM
January 5, 1979[33]

The letter is indeed fierce and mother Church took note of both the tone and the content, and the two priests became, from that moment onwards, stained with the mark of the ecclesiastical Cain. However, they did more: in the Lesotho Diocesan Synod of 1979, Michael and John were able to have a motion passed in support of the Program to combat racism and the Special Fund. They also organized for a collection to be taken at the Synod, to be sent to the Special Fund as a contribution from the Diocese of Lesotho.

---

[33] Michael Lapsley and John Osmers, "An open letter to the Archbishop and Bishops of the CPSA Re: The World Council of Churches Program to Combat Racism Special Fund."

❦CHAPTER 3

Lesotho

Few can deny that Lesotho is a very strange place. When you cross the border from South Africa, you enter a different world. In the late 1970's, Lesotho was ruled by Leabua Jonathan and his Basotholand National Party (BNP), as it had been ruled since the 1960's. Leabua was a strange man. Put in power by South Africa (and the Roman Catholic Church), he eventually turned against his political master and gradually allowed more freedom and privileges to the arch enemies of the apartheid state, the ANC.

The ANC, in turn, badly needed a base such as Lesotho and was inclined to overlook some of Leabua's excesses and the internal lack of democracy, accepting the principle of noninvolvement in the host country's internal affairs. Laudable though such a principle might be, promoted as it was by the United Nations, it was not very easily understood. There were many who thought the ANC was simply licking the feet (or even worse) of the one who fed it — conniving, as it were, with a local oppressor in the cause of a broader liberation struggle.

Leabua allowed the ANC, certainly in the late 1970's, to do what it wanted and with as much protection and assistance as tiny Lesotho could offer. This was done largely for pure motives; the man had come to believe in the justice of the ANC cause, even though he was not about to follow suit in his own country. He turned a blind eye to training, allowed Lesotho passports to be issued to ANC exiles and allowed ANC people free access in and out of the country. There were certainly benefits: Lesotho gained international credibility and huge amounts of aid from countries such as Sweden. Massive grants were handed over by the United Nations because Lesotho was prepared to give shelter to refugees, as it became home to many of South Africa's fleeing children. In fact, I remember South African exiles, whom I met years later in London, saying that when they got homesick, it was for Lesotho that they yearned. Why?

Because it was there, for the very first time, that many of us were able to live a fairly normal life. For the first time, many of us were able to experience what life without apartheid might look like.

But there was also a price which had to be paid — the price of the most extraordinary insecurity.

Lesotho is a small, landlocked country, with only one neighbor, South Africa. It is generally mountainous and now largely unarable. It is dependent on South Africa in every way — for every liter of petrol, every can of paraffin, every candle, every matchstick. Despite this, the Basotho are fiercely independent. "We Basotho...," they begin, and you know you are going to get some long and drawn out story about some marginally interesting Basotho custom, told as though it is the most important thing in the whole world. Most Basotho fondly imagine that they are situated in the middle of the Atlantic Ocean, rather than in the middle of South Africa.

The country is staggeringly beautiful and staggeringly cruel. The mountains scrape the sky, the weather is brisk and biting. The people wear blankets in hot weather and in cold. Why? "We Basotho..." (Even Basotho blankets are made in South Africa.) The story begins with a mountain, Thaba Bosiu — The Mountain of the Night. The legend is that the mountain is supposed to grow in the night. King Moshoeshoe I gathered together a motley band of refugees fleeing despots to the left and right and bound them into a nation.

Lesotho is a proud nation, but one with not a great deal going for it. In the nineteenth century, Lesotho used to export grain to the Orange Free State — the surrounding South African Province, but that was soon stopped. Now the country is simply eroding away through lack of land, little living space and bad farming methods. It is an aid agency paradise, with an abundance of arrogant and ignorant expatriates tramping the country from border to border showing the people how things should be done. Of course, the Basotho don't take the slightest notice. They just carry on, sliding deeper and deeper into poverty and dependency.

However, it is not all doom and gloom. Maseru (described as a "dusty little town" in the tourist brochures) has a certain curious charm of its own. There is a five star hotel on the hill overlooking the poverty, where white farmers from South Africa used to come and watch porn movies and sleep with black women. These days this recreation is available in Bloemfontein itself, so they don't come anymore.

The taxi rides to and from town are something beyond all imagination. The roads are extremely bad, but everyone has a sense of humor about it all. Time has a different meaning here: *Nako ea Afrika* (the time of Africa), which translated means very, very late and not giving a damn. It is a wonderful thing. You can be told that a church service will be taking place at 10:00 a.m. in the morning. You arrive half an hour before the appointed time. No one is there. 11 o'clock comes and goes. Then 12 noon. Possibly at about 12:45 p.m. some people arrive. The service gets underway at about 1:30 p.m. The absolute beauty of the situation is that no one worries.

The Church is a very important feature of Basotho life; virtually the whole country is Christian with the great majority being Roman Catholic. The Catholic Church could operate, by and large, as though no one else is there because of its numbers. It is therefore curious that it does not. Lesotho is one of the few countries in the region which can boast full Roman Catholic participation in the ecumenical Christian Council of Lesotho, the counterpart of the South African Council of Churches. However, most of the really impressive work of the Church is not done through the Council, but through a body called the "Heads of Churches." It is extraordinary that a country, rare in Africa to be blessed with one culture and one language, should be thoroughly divided denominationally. The missionaries certainly did a good job.

The combination of religiosity and the all pervasiveness of Basotho traditional culture dominates almost every weekend, when people scramble from one part of the country to the other, attending the funeral of this relative, or that. (Everyone in Lesotho is related to everyone, in one way or another.) The churches are full Sunday by Sunday. The Church is respected, even revered. The missionaries did a *very* good job.

Despite its relatively small size, the Anglican Church in Lesotho holds a place of respect and importance far in excess of its numbers. The Cathedral of St Mary and St James in Maseru is situated prominently, just behind the Palace. The King and the Anglican Bishop of Lesotho are near neighbors.

Desmond Tutu started his illustrious episcopal career as Bishop of Lesotho, the first black Anglican Bishop of Lesotho. Two things about his episcopate in Lesotho have etched themselves indelibly on the minds of the Basotho people: the first was that he left Lesotho after only eighteen months — a sin apparently never to be forgiven by the Diocese. In any case, during those eighteen months, he was apparently more out of the country than in it. The second notable fact about Bishop Desmond's time in Lesotho was that when he was Bishop, the Diocese was afloat with money; but when he left, so did most of the flow of external funds. This says more about the whims of the funders than Desmond Tutu. It is true, however, that he attracted a great deal of attention, monetary and otherwise, wherever he went. He has a flair for grand style and he maintained this even in the depths of rural Lesotho. Desmond Tutu, like many other bishops of the CPSA, is a Prince-Bishop of the Church with all that this entails. There is, of course, the other side to the man, a great and laudable side: the pastor, who traveled for miles on horseback to chastise a priest for not treating his parishioners with the dignity they deserved. The man of laughter and delight. The episcopal imp with a prophetic calling. This is also Desmond Tutu.

Michael's entry into the Church in Lesotho was not un-problematic. The Church is, and was, a very settled and conservative place. That is, after all, almost the nature of the Church. Michael's Order had people in it with very established and very fixed ideas. It is certain that Michael's high profile and exposed political ideas did not accord well with the way in which the Southern African Province of the SSM functioned. Moreover, the Anglican Church in Lesotho is extremely conservative ecclesiastically. It is straight High Church Anglican. The servers all wear tatty lace cottas[1] over well-worn red cassocks. The priest wouldn't dream of celebrating in anything less than full Roman or Gothic gear. The smell of incense is almost in the wood of the pews themselves, mixed intoxicatingly with woodsmoke and dust. Deacons wear dalmatics.[2] I even saw a sub-deacon (or someone parading as one) wearing a Humeral[3] once. I thought both had died a natural death, but no, here they both were, alive and well, and unaffected by the liturgical movement. There is much bell ringing and genuflection. Everyone clerical in sight wears

[1] Shortened form of the surplice, with less ample sleeves and a square cut yoke at the neck.
[2] Tunic ornamented with two colored strips running from front to back over the shoulders.
[3] Humeral veil is a silk shawl worn round the shoulders of the subdeacon at High Mass to serve as a covering for the hands while holding the paten. It is also worn sometimes by the celebrant in processions of the blessed Sacrament and during the service of Benediction.

copes and heads bow reverently at the mention of the name of Jesus. Women, of course, wear hats.

The Church here is conservative; three hundred years of biblical scholarship have largely passed it by. Jesus continues to walk on his water and shoots off into heaven like a rocket. God operates from his heaven in the sky and we are all trying to get there after we "pass on" or "over," or whatever. The hymns, the sermons Sunday by Sunday, the catechisms, the penitential classes, the worship — all reflect this kind of religiosity and piety. No one complains; the situation is comfortable, settled, and the Church, in Edgar Brookes' words, is "tragically irrelevant"[4]— but then it was never intended to be relevant, or at least not Relevant with a capital "R." Indeed is it not doing precisely what it should be doing? The people who flock to the churches of Lesotho are probably only marginally in fear of the loss of eternal life. The Church serves a purpose. It has a resonance in the very core of the people's identity. And what of it? Do the people want a relevant Church? Probably not. They want religion. They want familiar sounds and smells and thoughts. They want peace and a place to run to. They don't want to be challenged. Why should they? In largely rural Lesotho, they want somewhere to go to on a Sunday where they can wear something special.

Michael, to a very great degree, understood all of this. Perhaps in all of this were the glimmerings of his own religiosity. In many ways, Michael is a fairly traditional Anglo-catholic. He likes doing things "the right way." He knows when to genuflect and how to. He knew which thumb needs to cross which thumb when you clasp your hands together and walk in priestly procession. He knows what goes where and what this means and what that means. In fact, he prides himself on it. This is not the whole of his religion, but it is a very significant part of it. Michael is naturally religious, being one of those people for whom it is natural to believe. That is not to say that it is not difficult, and fraught with contradictions and all the rest of it. But it is natural for him, and the rest flows from that. Therefore, when Michael was placed in charge of the Ordinands at Lelapa la Jesu Seminary, it was something which he took to very easily.

The Seminary is a curious little affair, situated in the middle of the campus of the National University of Lesotho (NUL), in a little

---

[4] E. H. Brookes, "A Sword in the Hand of Christ," 1, in "The Universal Church in its South African setting," lectures delivered during Holy Week, 1966, in the Federal Theological Seminary in Alice, Eastern Cape, CPSA Archive, AB 847f.

town called Roma, about thirty kilometers to the south of Maseru. If Maseru is strange, Roma is stranger still. It is populated with Catholic institutions of one sort or another and awash with nuns and priests and Religious of every description. The university is small and populated with students mostly and numerous people looking for husbands and wives. The academic community of lecturers and professors is a tiny one; they all live together on the campus, attend each others parties, know about each other's affairs, and the world is very small and (in those days) very paranoid.

Michael had an amazing variety of friends on and off the campus: varied, different, interlocking, religious people, happy atheists, serious political activists, students, professors, sane, neurotic. Everyone knew Michael. Some liked him, some didn't. All in this little world in the middle of Africa, where foreign expatriates could come to live comfortably (with a salary being paid in the United States or Britain or wherever) and complain about things.

Michael lived at first in a rather large house on the seminary property, but he moved out into a much smaller one when a family needed the space. His house was extremely messy, especially the bedroom. Clothes would pile up until access became virtually impossible. Dishes accumulated in the kitchen. The house was always full of people, and Michael himself would not always know the guests in his house. They would come and go, stay for a while, leave, come back, do their ironing, cook, play music, listen to political tapes. Michael would come in and out as if he were another visitor. On one or two occasions, I saw him laying claim to his own space, but this was rare.

The walls were plastered with political posters, leaving one in no doubt as to his political allegiances. The whole place had the feel of a well-worn student digs. One extremely wealthy white woman was scandalized by a poster which Michael had hung on his front door, of the then President of SWAPO, Sam Nujoma, holding a baby with the caption underneath, "Survivors of a Colonial War." She wrote an angry letter to the Bishop, demanding that the poster be removed. The matter was discussed in the Bishop's Senate. John Osmers, who was at the time a member of the Bishop's Senate, said that he could not see the problem, as he was the one who had given Michael the poster! When Michael heard of the matter, he responded that he was equally, if not more affronted, by someone who owned Persian rugs so expensive that she could not bear to have them on the floor to be stepped on, but instead hung them on the walls —such was life in Lesotho!

There were some quite extraordinary visitors, such as Hilda, from New Zealand. Hilda was a rabid anti-apartheid activist who was rumoured to have stuck several flares up her rectum and led a demonstration on to the rugby pitch in New Zealand to protest against the South African Springboks' tour of the country. The flares, I believe, were part of the protest and were intended to be set off on the pitch. Whether they were, or not, I never heard. Hilda certainly was (is?) a character. She told the story of how she had been attacked during the protest by large, angry New Zealand men and physically beaten up. She recalled that her major concern at the time had been to stop them ripping her panties off — that was all she was worried about, not the beating on the head she was getting — to protect her dignity. Hilda was 60 plus if she was a day, with a deeply lined face and a husband left behind in New Zealand. She eventually taught at the John Maund school some thirty minutes from Roma in an even more remote part of the country. A more unlikely person to be working in that place, I never could have imagined.

Most people felt comfortable in Michael's house. There was a relaxed "African" feeling about the place.

My first encounter with Michael was very strange, and in a way he seemed very unlike the person I was to come to know later on. I was a young, green, ideologically confused, white (or so I thought then[5]) South African not wanting to go to the army. I had made a preliminary reconnaissance trip to Lesotho to try to organize a job and a place to live. I had been given Michael's name with the warning: "He's a card carrying member of the ANC." Those three dreaded letters breathed fear into the hearts and minds of white South Africa. When I first met him, he had had no warning of my arrival and was naturally a little suspicious. He was also damn rude. "Do you want tea or coffee?", he asked.

"Tea," I said timidly. "Tea?" he said incredulously. "Let me see, I think I had some here somewhere. I'll try to see if I can remember how to make it."

He slouched around the house in noisy "slops." He had long hair in those days, a Fidel Castro-type beard and a generally left-over hippy-type look. It was 5:00 p.m.: time for Mass. He quickly threw

---

[5] Like many "white" South Africans, Worsnip later discovered he should have been classified by the apartheid system as "colored."

on a white habit, wound an unfamiliar looking and extremely long red girdle around his waist, attached a cross to it, and marched off towards the chapel having exchanged his "slops" for running shoes. It was all rather bewildering.

When he returned he made two remarks that floored me. "So you don't want to go into the SADF?" he asked. "Then why don't you go into the other army?" Let me be honest: I did not even consider that there was another army. I imagined that *Umkhonto We Sizwe* was about 70 (or so) "terrorists" standing on "the border" (wherever that was) armed with Russian-made AK47's and limpet mines. I had no conception of what that "other army" might look like and I certainly had never considered joining it.

The second thing he said, quite casually in conversation, was a reference to "when *we* blew up Sasol."[6] I had never before met anyone who confessed to the blowing up of anything, let alone Sasol. To me, up to that point, it was always "them" and "they." The thought of "them" suddenly sitting in front of me and owning a deed such as this and talking about "we" and "us" was rather frightening, to say the least.

In a very short while after his arrival in Lesotho, Michael received a letter from the liaison Bishop to Chaplains, the then Bishop of Pretoria, Michael Nuttall. The students of the Anglican Students' Federation (ASF) had asked Michael to continue in Lesotho as National Chaplain-in-Exile. The Bishop seemed to take some exception to this. He complained about Michael's "open use of the title 'National Chaplain-in-exile'":

> I question the wisdom of this. You will remember my advice to you, that if you remained as National Chaplain, it should be on a low profile, without escalating the decision into a grand gesture, which would tend to draw attention to yourself rather than place the emphasis where it belonged, namely the continuity of the work...
>
> Another thought is that, although your permit to stay in South Africa was withdrawn (this, in my judgement, is not, strictly speaking, exile), you are still within the Province of Southern Africa and therefore still within the ASF constituency which is, of course, wider than the Republic...

---

[6] Sasol was, at the time, South Africa's most well-protected coal to oil conversion installation.

My counsel, therefore, is that you remain, simply and quietly, as National Chaplain (without the "exile" flourish), because that is what you are and that is what many of the students want you to be. [7]

The Bishop had other "concerns" which were "more complicated" and which were less easy to "express in detail in a letter." A concern about Michael's use of "certain phrases and ideas without any specifically Christian qualifications. You use in your press statement, phrases and even sentences (such as the last one — 'I express my solidarity with all the people as they struggle for a free and just society') which could serve a humanist or a Marxist equally well... We have to be absolutely God-centered and Christocentric, I believe, in all we say and do, and this is especially so if we are in positions of leadership."[8]

Michael was galled and wrote back immediately: "I think that you are incorrect when you state that in your judgement I am not in exile. It is true that I am not exiled from the Church of the Province, but whether or not you like the term (and it appears you don't) I am effectively in exile from the place where my community had asked me to live and I am prevented from living there by executive action of the SA [government]. Thus I remain in exile in the minds of most of the members of the ASF who live in the Republic."[9]

While he agreed with the Bishop that Christian leaders should be God-centered and Christ-centered, he felt nonetheless that the more searching question was what the terms meant: "What are the implications of the Incarnation? ...Isn't it also possible that something of the prophetic word of God comes to us from the humanists and the Marxists? We seem so often as Christians to try to limit the Truth of God... It is often my experience in the universities, particularly on the Black campuses, that the way in which some Christians say they are being God-centered, is a primary cause for the out of hand rejection of the gospel as irrelevant."[10]

He ended the letter by saying that he felt it was more important "to say what we think than [to] pretend, or be falsely polite." The Bishop replied, saying that they "would simply have to agree to

---

[7] The Rt Revd M. Nuttall, letter to Michael Lapsley, November 4, 1976.
[8] Ibid.
[9] Michael Lapsley, letter to The Rt Revd M. Nuttall, November 19, 1976.
[10] Ibid.

differ about certain things" and that he was "unwilling to become involved in lengthy debate by correspondence."[11]

By early 1979, Michael's deepened commitment to the ANC was beginning to make him wonder whether or not he should continue within the institutional Church in the way he had been up until that point. He had been appointed warden of the Seminary in Roma, having taken over the post from Donald Nestor, who had been elected Suffragan Bishop of Lesotho. In many ways it was a job which suited Michael well, enabling him to continue his good relationship with students on the university campus as well as being involved, in a creative way, with the formation of ordinands. It also allowed him the space to work closely with ANC structures on the campus and this had the effect of broadening and deepening his political analysis of the situation in the subregion. For Michael, it was an early realization that the individual prophetic personality was no threat at all to the apartheid state. Individuals could come and could go and the state could merrily ignore the whole lot of them, or even gain credibility by allowing their continued existence. But when one joined a movement, particularly a mass movement such as the ANC — that was a very different matter.

It was with this understanding that Michael accepted a teaching post at the ANC's Solomon Mahlangu Freedom College at Mazimbu in Tanzania from the end of May 1980. He wrote a letter of resignation, more than a year before his departure date, to the Bishop of Lesotho in the following terms:

> It is my belief that the African National Congress of South Africa (ANC) based on the Freedom Charter adopted at the Congress of the People in 1955, most clearly incarnates the social and political implications of the Christian gospel in South Africa. At this stage, as a person, as a priest and a member of a Religious Order, I believe that the most godly thing that I can do is to put myself at the service of the ANC and from within this organization and mass liberation movement, strive to make my contribution towards the struggle for a society where we can all be more truly brothers and sisters...
>
> I understand that the CPSA at Provincial Synod and at the Synod of Bishops accepts that some of its members may in obedience to the gospel, join liberation movements and that

---

[11] The Rt Revd M. Nuttall, letter to Michael Lapsley, December 13, 1976.

also the Church has a responsibility to minister to members of the liberation movement.[12]

Michael had, in fact, checked this idea out with both SSM and the Diocese of Lesotho. The Bishop had, after some hesitation, agreed to allow Michael to do what he believed the Spirit was leading him to do. The SSM too, had agreed. Then came the personal intervention of the then President of the ANC, Oliver Tambo. Hearing of Michael's planned relocation to Mazimbu, Tambo refused to allow him to do it, on the grounds that he was far more valuable to the ANC in the position which he held in Roma, than he ever could be in Tanzania.

Michael was now clearly in a bit of a fix, having convinced both the Diocese and his Order to allow him to move, and with their blessing, he now needed to convince them that he should stay — again with their blessing. Bishop Philip Mokuku noted wryly that the wishes of the Holy Spirit and those of Oliver Tambo seemed to be somewhat indistinguishable on this occasion. Nevertheless, all parties eventually agreed that Michael should stay.

Michael's house on the seminary property had become a meeting place for all kinds of people on the campus. On one occasion, I believe, a meeting was held in the bathroom, because there were meetings taking place in every other room. It was also beginning to gain something of a reputation as an "ANC center," which, of course, it never was.

Given the level of paranoia about the ANC in those days, it is not difficult to understand what motivated this idea. People were very scared, and they had good reason to be scared. The apartheid regime was, with gay abandon, crossing any border it chose in order to kill or attack its opponents. The message was clearly: "Beware of anyone in the ANC." "If you are not careful, you could end up dead." It was a message which didn't need a great deal of elaboration: "Card-carrying members of the ANC" were dangerous people, and Michael was to be counted among their number. He would certainly have understood what he was doing as both a ministry to refugees and a participant in the liberation struggle of the people. But others would simply have seen the danger and this would override all other considerations.

---

[12] Michael Lapsley, letter to The Rt Revd P. Mokuku, February 20, 1979.

A *Sunday Express* reporter visited Roma in February 1982 in search of student leader Sammy Adelman, who had fled South Africa for Lesotho. She interviewed Michael in the seminary and reported the interview in the following terms:

> Father Mike Lupsly (sic) runs the sophisticated Christian Center/ANC-supporters refugee camp, on the Lesotho University Campus. During a meeting in his flat this week, he was very cagey about discussing Mr Adelman whom he saw earlier this week.
>
> His first comments to us were "Why are my South African brothers taking so long about bringing on the revolution?"
>
> Then he agreed to talk about Sammy Adelman.
>
> "I have no idea where he is staying. He is being very closely guarded. There are many South African spies in Lesotho and he must be protected from them," Mr Lupsly (sic) said.[13]

Michael immediately issued a denial, denouncing the report as "largely fictitious" and bringing into question "the intentions, integrity and credibility" of the *Sunday Express*:

> The report... alleges that I run the "sophisticated Christian Center/ANC-supporters refugee camp on campus." At the Anglican Center we are training four Basotho and one Swazi for the priesthood. On our premises there is also a nursery school and children's library. In the light of your government's threats and actions against refugees, we hope that the wild allegations of your newspaper have not put the lives of seminarians, priests or students in danger.[14]

In March of the same year, *The Citizen* newspaper (owned and run by state interests) ran an article entitled "Priest who is an ANC

---

[13] C. Pretorius, "Cat and mouse life of SA student fugitive," *Sunday Express*, February 21, 1982.

[14] Telegram, February 26, 1982. Some of the text of the telegram was reproduced in the following week's edition of the *Sunday Express*, see "Priest denies student refugee report," *Sunday Express*, March 7, 1982.

propagandist"[15] by one Aida Tarter (actually Aida Parker of the "Aida Parker Newsletter" — a purportedly "Christian" publication which usually served the interests of the rightwing by publishing fiercely anti-communist views for Christian readership). There was not a great deal novel in the article; it proceeds along well-worn paths — anti-World Council of Churches; anti-Liberation Theology; anti-Anglican Church; anti-South African Council of Churches and then quoting the *Wall Street Journal* as the final and authoritative voice of reason as well as theology and everything else. The article was nothing more than a crude attack on Michael, but it showed that eyes were on him, particularly in Pretoria. Michael was not unduly concerned by such articles; he continued to check under his car for bombs. Life continued very much as normal.

Michael was on holiday in New Zealand on December 9, 1982. Those of us who were in Roma, thirty minutes out of Maseru, woke to the scratchy voice of radio announcer Bea Reed, telling us that the South African Defense Forces had launched a pre-emptive attack on "terrorist" bases in Maseru. A number of targets had been hit and the mission was declared successful. People in Maseru already knew what had happened, having being woken by the sounds of the shooting, firebombing and helicopters the previous night.

As we leapt into the car that morning and drove towards Maseru, we could not but wonder which of our friends was alive. We saw two students whom we knew well, ANC black students — Tito and Ngoako[16] — outside the university, hitching a ride in to Maseru. They too had only just heard the news, and as we traveled together, like the travelers on the road to Emmaus, we despaired at what we saw. Look at that house! Blackened walls and door frame. What about comrade A's house? Yes, it was gone. And this one? They missed that! Look there! Oh my God! They got him, too.

They hit comrade Chris Hani's[17] house — but he had moved two weeks previous, and was not even in the country. Surely the people inside must be dead.

---

[15] *The Citizen*, March 30, 1982. A longer version of the article appeared in *The Aida Parker Newsletter*, October 13, 1983, entitled "Killing for Christ: One 'priest's' crusade boosts ANC terror."

[16] Tito Mboweni and Ngoako Ramahloli, now the Minister of Labor and the Premier of the Northern Province respectively.

[17] Chris Hani was Chief of Staff of Umkhonto We Sizwe. He became the leader of the South African Communist Party and was assassinated in April 1993.

In the face of this devastation, what now? We must pick up the spear where it has fallen. "Now, comrades," they said to us, "we must fight harder than ever before. Now is not the time to despair. Now is the time to stand up and be counted."

Those words will live with me forever. The sight of those blackened houses, ordinary civilian houses with ordinary civilian refugees living in them, will always haunt me — their roofs blown out, their windows broken and their contents of bloodied, dismembered, dead, men, women, children — some of whom had been asleep in their beds.

ONS SAL LEWE ONS SAL STERWE, ONS VIR JOU SUID AFRIKA. (We will live, we will die, we are for you, South Africa.) These are the words of the apartheid state's anthem.

The devastation was indescribable. The sense of having been raped was almost tangible; the city had been raped, as had the country. And there was not a damned thing anyone could do about it. Lesotho had a joke for an army, completely dependent and totally vulnerable to attack. Of course, international protests could be made at the highest levels and people could shake their heads and their fists in anger. But the apartheid state would simply act with impunity. Twelve Basotho nationals were "killed in the crossfire" is what they said. One Mosotho had her throat slashed; another was killed because the attackers counted windows from the wrong side of the building before hitting it. A hotel in the middle of town was riddled with Boer bullets.

Of course people were frightened. The raid was not only meant to kill, it was meant to terrorize an entire nation and it did. For some, however, it meant the need for greater resolve and even greater commitment.

Not so the Church. There we sing: "Let courage rise with danger." God knows what we mean by it. The Senate of the Anglican Church of Lesotho, meeting some five days after the massacre came to the conclusion that because of Michael's opposition to apartheid, his work amongst the refugee population and his open membership of the ANC, he was a potential target for the South African government. Convinced by what it perceived to be a danger to Michael's life, as well as a danger to those around him, the Senate advised the Bishop to write to him in New Zealand and tell him not to return to his post in Lesotho. The Bishop did so, some nineteen days later (*Nako ea Africa!*), in the following terms:

I hope that you are well and that you have rested and had a good time with your family. I know that your thoughts and prayers will have been much in Lesotho, especially with the refugees just after the South African raid on Maseru.

The raid has caused great distress and fear, quite apart from the appalling loss of life, not only among the refugee community, but also among ordinary Basotho. After discussing the matter fully in Senate, I am sorry to tell you that I believe it would not be right for you to return to Lesotho as planned... Since this is bound to cause you some difficulties, I feel I should go into the reasons for this decision, which has not been taken lightly.

There is the harm, both actual and to a much greater degree potential, which comes to our seminary residence at Roma, and therefore to the Church as a whole. The Church of Jesus Christ has to be a haven for those in distress, that is in this case, the refugees, but the position of our residence at Roma is not simply a haven for refugees.... I have never failed to point out that it is our obligation as shepherds of the flock of Christ to be sensitive and to be seen to be sensitive, to people of different political allegiances, and those who are not particularly interested in politics. This is not to say that people's political awareness should not be sharpened. The question is how this is to be done, and in my opinion it must not be done in too partisan a way by one who is supposed to be a shepherd to all his flock.

...One thing that hardly needs emphasising is that the decision to ask you not to return to Lesotho as planned has not been taken lightly Michael, we have taken this decision because of the danger that would face Lelapa la Jesu as well as your own life if you return.[18]

Michael arrived back in Lesotho on Saturday, January 15, 1983, never having received the letter. He was met at the airport by the Bishop suffragan, Donald Nestor; the Provincial of his Order, Clement Mullinger; and the Prior of the Masite house of SSM, David Wells. They asked Michael to accompany them to Clement Mullinger's house, where they presented him with a copy of two letters which had been sent to him in New Zealand, neither of which

---

[18] The Rt Revd P. Mokuku, letter to Michael Lapsley, December 28, 1982.

he had received. Michael was deeply shocked. "I had half expected something like that from the government, but not from the Church."[19] However, perhaps the greatest shock was still to come when David Wells told Michael that the brothers at Masite had resolved unanimously that he would not be allowed to sleep under the same roof as the community. Even though the community had allowed other ANC refugees to stay after the raid, they were unanimous in their agreement not to have Michael. When Michael said that the sisters at Masite had offered him hospitality, David Wells said that he was their warden and he would tell them not to allow Michael to sleep there.[20]

Michael returned that evening to Roma and informed the priest who had been officiating in his absence that he had now returned from leave and that he would be saying Mass the following day. At the Mass, Michael told the congregation about the letters and suggested that this was not the moment to respond to them. He expressed the wish that they, the congregation, would be consulted before any final decision was made.

On the Monday, Michael met with Bishop Donald Nestor, who was Vicar-General since the Diocesan, Bishop Mokuku, was away in the United Kingdom at the time. The Bishop was extremely angry with Michael for having returned to Roma at all and said that Michael should have understood that he was no longer chaplain to the university, nor the parish priest and was therefore not supposed to go to Roma. The Bishop was then joined by the Provincial of SSM who said that he felt being a member of the SSM and the ANC were incompatible.

Michael decided to appeal against the ruling: he asked to meet with the Senate, whose decision it had been to ask him not to return. On the Wednesday afternoon, they met. Michael's case was fairly straightforward: he argued that he had come to Lesotho because of apartheid and now he was being forced to leave because of apartheid,

---

[19] Michael Lapsley, "Report to ANC," January 24, 1983.
[20] Ibid. See also Michael Lapsley, "A letter to the brothers of the Southern African Province of the Society of the Sacred Mission," May 25, 1984. It needs to be said, however, that David Wells was also one of the first to be at Michael's bedside after the bomb, besides accompanying him all the way to Australia when he needed to transfer hospitals. In many ways, David has been a real brother to Michael. I record this incident, however, to show the extreme rejection which Michael faced.

only this time through the action of the Church. In this respect the Church was unconsciously doing Pretoria's work for it by getting rid of him.

However, this was not the only motivation. The previous year two of the white CPSA bishops had attacked Michael and threatened not to send any further students to the seminary if he were to continue as warden. A significant card was being played here: at that time, there was a somewhat undignified scramble for theological students throughout the Province. Several Dioceses had decided to "go it alone" and train students themselves, while others tended to use their students like jackpot vouchers. Generally, it was all a charade, because students would normally be sent to "safe" colleges anyway, if they were sent anywhere at all. This was therefore a direct threat levelled at Michael's position, not because of his moral stature, nor because of his lifestyle, but because he dared to align himself with mainstream political thinking in the region and openly support the ANC.

The Bishops of Lesotho, to their enduring credit, supported Michael and stated clearly at the time that Michael was appointed to the position because of the confidence they had in him as a person and as a priest.[21] It should be noted that the same white bishops in South Africa appear not to have had problems about sending their candidates to other colleges where the staff were members of white political parties or who had done military training in the South African Defense Force. This was not even thought of as an issue worthy of consideration.[22]

Michael spoke of ANC refugees who were being thrown out of their houses in Maseru. "What is the Church saying about this?" Michael asked the Senate. He drew the obvious parallel between what was happening in Lesotho and what had happened in Germany in the 1930's. People said that the problem then was the Jews. They did not seem to think that the problem might be Hitler. Michael argued that this was not the time to be seen to be withdrawing. He was, after all, the only Church person working with refugees in Lesotho at the time and he had been doing this all along with the approval of the Senate.

---

[21] Michael Lapsley, letter to The Most Revd P. Russell, April 3, 1983.
[22] See Michael Lapsley, "Statement," March 3, 1983, 1. See also "Protests over 'sacked' Lesotho Chaplain" in *Seek*, March 1983.

The Senate then briefly discussed the issue of two other ANC refugees who were living at the seminary and said that they should be encouraged to look for alternative accommodation. Whatever happened, people were going to feel offended, said the members. It was clear to the members, however, that Michael could not be allowed to stay in Roma. He would be given one month to say his goodbyes in the Diocese, which could not offer him any other work. Michael had to recognize the danger he was to other people.

On the Thursday morning, he met with the brethren of the SSM. They argued as follows: There is a rumour that the Boers want to get Michael, therefore he should leave immediately because of the risk, even if this were only for a short time.

Michael should consider other parts of Africa where things are very bad. South Africa at least would not be as bad as the rest of Africa. One brother from the Free State stated that he had considerable difficulty sitting in the same room as someone who was committed to murder. Michael was asked if he supported terrorism.

It was strongly suggested that he should not appeal to the stipulation in Canon Law which allows for a three month period before removal, but that he should leave as soon as possible.

On the Friday morning, Michael met again with the Bishops and the Dean, Fr Israel Qwelane, to make his response to the Wednesday meeting with the Senate. Michael considered the issue of the danger, recalling the bomb which had been sent to John Osmers which was addressed to the Masite Mission. Were the people then not in danger? Yet John was warmly welcomed back to Lesotho. (John Osmers was subsequently deported in absentia from Lesotho by the government.) The point was made over and over again, that while Michael himself might be willing to accept the danger, the bullets and the bombs might well hit someone else.

Bishop Donald now said that he had spoken to the priest at Roma and that he had concluded that Michael could not stay at Roma for a month, as had been previously suggested. The reason for this was that people at Roma were supporting Michael and making all kinds of accusations against the Church. If Michael were to return to Roma, the life of the priest who had replaced Michael, together with his wife and family, would be in danger.

Michael reminded the Bishop that under Canon law, he could not get rid of him in such a summary manner and was bound to give him three months' notice. The Bishop replied that he would find another law.[23] The Bishop also said that he would be coming to Roma to speak to the congregation that Sunday, but that Michael was not allowed to be present at the service, because if he were present he would want to state his case before the congregation. The Dean said that this was unreasonable on the part of the Bishop.

Michael then said that he felt that the problem was really about his ANC membership: the Church was forcing him to make false choices, and therefore he wanted permission to travel immediately to Lusaka, Zambia, to consult with the ANC.

At the Sunday Mass in the Roma Chaplaincy, Bishop Donald was present in order to discuss the matter of Michael's dismissal with the congregation in Roma. Many protested strongly about the way in which Michael had been treated, including the fact that he was not being permitted to speak on that occasion, and that the congregation had not been consulted. The danger was something people had already been aware of and many could not understand why all of a sudden the authorities had decided to act in this way.

Numerous protests were received from many quarters, including members of the congregation which Michael served, both black and white.[24] The letter which the members of the congregation wrote expressed the view that the decision to dismiss Michael was "in stark contrast" to the debate which took place in the Provincial Synod the previous year about ministry to refugees. The members found it "incomprehensible" that one of the very few priests working in this area should be removed because of fears for his personal safety, without consulting him. They were surprised that he was being dismissed "without notice and in absentia." Of all the letters written and received, perhaps none was as direct and emotional as that which Bishop Philip received from Phyllis Naidoo:

> Philip,
>
> When I called to see you and you were asleep that morning and when I spoke to Nestor he said that your church was afraid for Mike's safety.
>
> You phoned later and confirmed that fear. You also said that it was the decision of the Senate... and that you were not

---

[23] Michael Lapsley, letter to The Most Revd P. Russell, April 3, 1983.
[24] C. Obol et al, letter addressed to the Archbishop of Cape Town and the Bishops of the CPSA, February 4, 1983.

present. All the while I was under the impression that it was some priests/bishops from the Republic whose support for the racist regime and its policies made Mike an anathema in their midst with his pro-liberation stand. I had no idea that it was his brothers here that had worked with him!

Mike came to this country in 1976 when the racists deported him... Some say that it was easy for a man like Mike with a New Zealand passport to move off and leave those who stay behind to face the music. But that music we face is the liberation struggle to which we have dedicated our lives...

The Lesotho Church accepted him. He was then partisan. He had chosen on his own volition the side of the oppressed. And only the oppressed know the difficulty of their oppression. We were and continue to be proud that a foreigner had opted for our cause and opted to share the trials of our oppression. Do you understand that Philip? He is a very proud addition to our family, for he chose a difficult path. It is so easy and comfortable not to move a finger in the face of oppression and thrust it upon the good Lord and to pray for him to remove the oppression that has been the lot of my people for over 300 years, nay then, the Church has actively contributed to that oppression, using the Bible to justify their position... You will pardon me, for my heart is there with Mike alone amongst his brothers. Philip, when you told me you were making representations to the [government] to get John Osmers back to Lesotho, did you? Did you? Were you happy/relieved that the government had done your work for you? He was partisan too. He was a member of the ANC. Were you afraid for him? He was parcel-bombed and lost his hand and suffered severe injuries. His safety had never been in issue had it Philip? Dear Bishop you would not have lied to me would you? You did make representations to the government. I saw you after several of your meetings with the government. I believe that you did see them. The issue of his safety, my brother John, never came up. You were, Philip, doing your damnedest to get him back?

Ah yes, you will say, but we did not have the Maseru massacre then? But we did, you know Philip. Nearly 300 men, women and children (mainly children Philip) were murdered at Kassinga, in Chimoyo and Matola. Not to speak of the daily murders that happen in my country. You must know that anyone that opposes the racists next door is a communist, a terrorist and must be annihilated...

Why were you not concerned for John's safety — why only Mike?... Your letter tells more of your fears for Mike's safety [than] it speaks of... [the issue of partisanship]

Forgive me Philip, but my reading of your letter[25] makes this and and this alone the reason for my brother Mike's deportation from Lesotho... Has it taken the Church 5 years to appreciate his partisanship...? Why is the pressure on Mike now in 1983? His partisanship was public in 1977... Why is the membership of the ANC and the raid being treated together. Are these not separate issues. The one has been with the Church for 5 yrs publicly and the other with the bodies of my brothers and sisters hardly decomposed?

Has the raid been an excuse? If this is so then Philip this whole business is a terrible reflection on the Church. The Church which you head, my dear Philip...

I can say no more.

Phyllis[26]

The agreement which was finally reached between Michael and the Diocese was that he would leave Lesotho, without abandoning any positions of principle, although he would not insist on the three months which were legally due to him.[27] It is therefore difficult to understand the rationale behind a letter which then came from Bishop Donald Nestor, written two weeks after this agreement had been reached which read:

I hope that you are well and coping with clearing up your affairs at Roma...

Nevertheless I feel I must point out, as your Bishop and Father-in-God, that we have given you sufficient time to clear up your affairs. When I originally allowed you a month to do this, but then withdrew that offer and asked you to do it as soon as possible because of the difficulties which might be caused to our continuing work at Roma, I did not expect you

---

[25] The Rt Revd P. Mokuku, letter to Michael Lapsley, December 28, 1982
[26] Phyllis Naidoo, letter to The Rt Revd P. Mokuku, January 20, 1983.
[27] Lapsley, "Report to ANC."

to use the time to encourage (or not actively discourage) numerous press statements to appear. Naturally I would not want to prevent such freedom of expressions in a public forum... but these public statements have caused and are causing great difficulties to our work at Roma. I am merely pointing this out to you. I feel that we have allowed you more time than was needed to put your affairs in order, and that the time has been used for other purposes. I believe that you have caused much harm not only to the Church's work at Roma, but also to yourself and the refugees, whom we are just as concerned to help as you are yourself.

Please would you leave Roma as soon as possible, ideally by Monday, February 21, and at least before the following Sunday.[28]

Michael did not respond directly to this letter, as relations were beginning to sour dramatically. However, some months later, when he was appealing formally to the Archbishop against his dismissal, he deals with the accusation which the Bishop makes here.

Bishop Donald released a statement which became front page news in *The Friend, The Rand Daily Mail* and also appeared in *The Cape Times* as well as Lesotho papers and was quoted extensively on Radio Lesotho and reported on Capital Radio and Radio Five. People have also reported that it was heard as a news item on radio stations in different European countries. At this point Bishop Donald came to accuse me of being in some way behind the press coverage and said that there was now a scandal. Consequently I must finish packing and leave Roma within three days [because]... clearly I hadn't been packing but rather organizing responses to the Church's action... In the face of the protest and scandal, the Church comes to attack me again, instead of considering if there was something wrong in the decision itself as well as the manner of implementation. I cannot be blamed or held responsible for reactions to a decision about which it was not thought necessary to consult me. It is also insulting to those who felt

---

[28] The Rt Revd D. Nestor, letter to Michael Lapsley, February 18, 1983.

moved to make a response and protest to the Church about its actions.[29]

Michael was feeling extremely bewildered by the extent of the rejection he was experiencing. "I had the feeling that I was a criminal who had committed an indescribable crime," he reflected in the same letter. In his farewell sermon, he tries to make sense of this feeling by returning to the fundamentals of his faith:

To be a follower of Jesus is to have certain ways of viewing the world, of understanding what is to be done, of struggling to live by faith, hope and love, of having glimpses of who God is as he reveals himself, especially in poor people struggling to be free. Jesus loved to the limit, he was never intimidated. He died to free us all. He confronted all who oppressed others, especially the religious hypocrites of his day — those who parade their religion before people while ripping off the poor.

Times haven't changed very much. Jesus confronted the oppressive power structure of his day to the point that people had no choice. They either had to become his followers or they had to get rid of him. And today, it is the same. If you speak the truth too loudly, you must be gotten rid of. Either shot by the politician, or deported for your own safety by the religious people for the good of everyone around you....

The gospel of Jesus Christ confronts all that prevents us from developing our full human potential. All that offends against human dignity and the pursuit of liberation in all its forms. However, not surprisingly, the kind of religion which seems to be becoming daily more popular on this campus [is]... a kind of opium, a kind of spirituality which soothes us and keeps us in a cocoon but does not confront the issues of our campus or even of our day....

An impression has been created in this campus community that social justice and the pursuit of liberation is the preserve of the communist and the anti-religious which no God-fearing man or woman should soil their hands with. What a tragedy and what a travesty of the Christ event, which ends once and for all these divisions between the sacred and the secular....

---

[29] Michael Lapsley, letter to The Most Revd P. Russell, April 3, 1983.

The test of our religion is not the frequency of our Mass-going, but how we treat the most oppressed and whether we ourselves are the oppressors of others....

Those on this campus who are, in some sense, not antagonistic but unsympathetic to the Christian faith will often dismiss our faith as idealistic... But they have not read the gospel [which we heard read today]... There could hardly be a more materialistic gospel than what we heard read today. Jesus is saying, "You are not going to find me in the sky. I'm not there in the sky. I'm in the poor. I'm in the hungry. I'm naked, in prison. If you are not going to find me there, you are not going to find me anywhere else."...How much are we willing to put our lives on the line for those at the bottom?... Whose side are we on?... [S]o often those in power in the Church have said that Jesus Christ didn't take sides. I want to suggest that all of us [should] read the gospel again. Not my gospel, but the one in the book, and see whether or not Jesus Christ hasn't in fact taken sides with those on the bottom. Whoever they are, whether they are black, or because they are poor, or because they are women or whatever the reason.

You see, the Church of God, or should I say the Church as an institution, won't die tomorrow in Lesotho or South Africa. But it may become irrelevant. And as the blood flows on the streets, if we close the doors more and more securely and sing our hymns more and more loudly, the blood won't go away.

We have a promise as Christians, from the one we seek to follow. The promise is not that things will be a bed of roses, but that he will be with us. That is the promise we have. And we shouldn't be surprised, if we seek to follow Jesus, that it will cost us our lives. It cost him his life. And we shouldn't be afraid, as Christians, to join other people of goodwill. Jesus himself chose so frequently not to make common cause with the religious people of his day. He chose to make common cause with people of goodwill, who sought a new society, a vision, a hope for the future.[30]

The tone of the sermon is somber and subdued. But within it there is also a confidence and a certainty. Michael has no doubt whatsoever

---

[30] Michael Lapsley, sermon, "What is to be done?", February 20, 1983.

that he is correct, theologically, about the stand which he is taking; he has no doubt that the path he has chosen is right and just; and he has no doubt that the Church is behaving in a way which is weak and duplicitous. What he cannot understand — indeed it is extremely difficult to understand — is why he is being treated so badly. His letter to (then) Archbishop Philip Russell in which he appeals against his dismissal expresses some of his feelings of alienation, rejection and pain:

> I could not help feeling ashamed of the Bishops of Lesotho and some of my brother priests and members of my own community because of what they had done.
>
> However, I appeal not just because of my personal feelings, but also because I believe that what has been done to me as a response to the massacre has some significance in the working out of the Church's relation to the struggle for liberation in Southern Africa. Does our faith not require us to make common cause with those who seek to end apartheid and create a human society in Southern Africa?[31]

The remark about being "ashamed of the Bishops of Lesotho" angered Bishop Donald considerably, who then wrote Michael a personal letter on the basis of "friendship over many years." Statements like this, the Bishop suggested, made it "difficult for us as leaders of the Church in Lesotho to welcome you back with open arms at present." The Bishop also felt that Michael's "manner" and "approach to people who feel differently" from himself was often "provocative and confrontational." He felt that this was resented, both by "many Basotho" and others. While it might be permissible in a university setting with articulate students and staff, generally even there, it is resented. "You can be, and have been, such a sensitive person, that to see you so often hurting people when you are engaged in a dialogue with them is very sad." The Bishop continued:

> We have been hurt and I personally have been hurt, as I know you have been. But where I believe we had to act is where we see that other people for whom we were responsible are being

---

[31] Michael Lapsley, letter to The Most Revd P. Russell, April 3, 1983

hurt by your actions. I believe even more strongly that you yourself are being hurt by your own actions....

I can allow you to feel that you owed your self-value as a person to make your appeal, and to do it in the way you did. But now I am appealing to you to feel that you owe it to yourself also to stop hurting others, and as a result to stop hurting yourself and your cause.[32]

It was an excruciatingly patronizing letter which could have done nothing at all to improve the situation. In fact it succeeded in worsening it considerably, because the Bishop then wrote to the Archbishop telling him that he had appealed to Michael to "stop hurting himself and them." Michael, after having written several letters to the Archbishop himself, asking how far his appeal had gone, eventually received a letter, not from the Archbishop, but from the Provincial Executive Officer, Bishop Amoore, who described Bishop Donald's letter to Michael as "the most helpful thing" which had happened.[33] Michael responded:

I am not sure how the contents of a letter which purported to be written on "a personal level of friendship" from Bishop Nestor to me can now become "the most helpful thing" in correspondence between you as Archbishop and myself concerning my dismissal by the Diocese of Lesotho....

I addressed my appeal to you as Archbishop more than three months ago because I believed that a decision had been taken against me which was not only unjust and uncanonical but which had brought the name of the Diocese of Lesotho and the Church of the Province of Southern Africa into disrepute in Lesotho and abroad.

When, three months later, a decision which I was not involved in making has still not been rescinded, I am appealed to, "to stop hurting yourself and them," I cannot help feeling that a situation has been turned on its head. Is it reasonable (or even addressed to the right quarter) to appeal to the one dismissed to "stop hurting himself" and those who have

---

[32] The Rt Revd D. Nestor, letter to Michael Lapsley, May 19, 1983.
[33] The Rt Revd F. Amoore, letter to Michael Lapsley, July 12, 1983.

dismissed him, whilst even the outcome of an appeal is still unknown?[34]

After seven months and four letters from Michael addressed directly to the Archbishop, he still had not heard the result of his appeal, nor had he heard directly from the Archbishop, nor had he been informed as to what procedure the Archbishop would follow in order to evaluate the appeal. Finally in late November, the Archbishop replied to Michael in the following terms:

> I have now been able to consider all the circumstances and the Canons... I have also consulted with the Provincial Registrar with reference to the legal interpretation of Canon 24, and he advises me that the Senate, having come unanimously to the conclusion that your services should be terminated and having advised the Vicar-General accordingly, the latter had no option but to act upon their advice. You were not present in Lesotho at the time, and so he wrote a pastoral letter to you which can be considered as pastoral ministration under the Canon in the circumstances.
>
> I have therefore come to the conclusion that your appeal must fail and I rule accordingly.[35]

Apart from the fact that a letter informing Michael that his services were no longer required by the Diocese and which he had never received in any case, should suddenly now become "pastoral ministration" (as was required under Canon 24), it is extraordinary that the Archbishop and Metropolitan of the Province, after a seven month delay in responding to Michael's position, should at this point adopt so formal and chilly a tone in his letter.

Michael's appeal had been on the grounds of unfair dismissal: that the Bishop did not have the power to summarily dismiss him in the way he did and that the Canons required that the priest be given three months' notice. This had not happened, and therefore he could not understand how, by what seemed to be archepiscopal decree, his appeal had simply "failed." He wrote a personal letter to the Archbishop. He wanted to clear up one issue which had been reported to him via two friends, Margaret Nash and Barney Pityana,

---

[34] Michael Lapsley, letter to The Most Revd P. Russell, July 22, 1983.
[35] The Most Revd P. Russell, letter to Michael Lapsley, November 24, 1983.

who had met the Archbishop and spoken to him. They both felt that the Archbishop had had "negative" feelings towards Michael since 1976, when Michael had reacted strongly to his lack of response to his deportation. Barney Pityana also indicated to Michael that the Archbishop felt that Michael had "too many masters":

> As far as too many masters are concerned all I can say is that I have tried to live my life with integrity. For me being a priest, a Religious, and participation in the liberation struggle have all been part of simply trying to be human in Southern Africa. I agree it can at times be very complicated, but I guess all human beings have problems of loyalties at times — to the Church, to the nation, to the gospel, to relatives, to oneself etc., and I am not unique, but they may appear at times particularly stark in my case. I have tried to be open and straight — my mistake, some would say.
>
> When I wrote to appeal in April of last year, I made a formal appeal — but I also shared some of my hurt and anger and hoped for both a formal and a pastoral response. It never came. Others told me that the bishops are a club who all stand together and I should not expect either justice or compassion. I believed I would get both from you but feel I have received neither.
>
> Donald kept telling me how much I was hurting the Church and how I should stop — but he remains a bishop and I remain dismissed and he wasn't willing to do anything about that. It seemed to me that the situation kept being turned on its head. I became the victim twice or thrice over. It was as if I had caused the massacre, it was my fault that I was dismissed, and my fault that people protested against it.[36]

Michael pointed out in the same letter that he felt that had he been a rapist or a murderer, he would have received more pastoral care from the Diocese and the Province than he had. What was his alleged crime? That in word and in deed he was totally opposed to apartheid and because of that, there was a danger that the South African government wanted to kill him. "Maybe," he wrote forlornly, "if I

---

[36] Michael Lapsley, letter to The Most Revd P. Russell, February 6, 1984.

was more holy, I would be able to accept what happened more easily." [37] The Archbishop's reply, a month later, read as follows:

> I would point out that Canon 24 provides for a right of appeal within two months of the date of the notice given. The notice to you was dated December 27, 1982, so that the right of appeal expired on February 26, 1983. Your letter of appeal dated April 3, 1983, was late. Nevertheless I did consider all you had written in connection with your appeal, and also received legal advice from the Provincial Registrar (confirmed by the Chancellor) upon which, as stated in my letter of November 24, I came to the conclusion that your appeal failed, and I ruled accordingly. There is no procedure by which you can take this matter further, and you must now accept that it is closed.
>
> On the point you raise about summary dismissal, you are quite correct that you were entitled to three months' notice but I was assured by the Diocese that you were paid to March 27, 1983, when that period expired.
>
> Yours sincerely
>
> + Philip Cape Town [38]

However, there was more to come, not from the CPSA, but from Michael's Order. In May 1984, Michael received a copy of the minutes of a meeting of the Provincial Chapter of SSM, which had been held in Maseru on December 29-30, 1983. They read as follows:

> The Provincial presented his report and asked for comment. Frank thought that there should be some addition in the section about Michael, insofar as the latter's presence was seen to be a threat to innocent people around. Anthony thought the "threat" business was overplayed. He saw Michael's actions (and presence) as being a matter of lack of obedience, and not merely a threat. Andrew said that Michael claimed obedience to an alien political organization. Mark said he had already put in writing through the Provincial to the Director

---

[37] Ibid.
[38] The Most Revd P. Russell, letter to Michael Lapsley, March 28, 1984.

his own view, namely that the taking up of arms in pursuit of this ideal, was not a position he could accept. He saw it as foreign to the Society's way of life and purpose. What was more important was not Michael's attitude to the Society, but the Society's attitude to Michael. Brethren queried whether this was not the time for the Director to consider asking Michael to remove from the Society.

The Chapter passed the following resolution:
This Chapter counsels the Director to look at the possibility of ordering Michael not to set foot on the African continent.

The Resolution was prefaced with the following:
Insofar as this Chapter is convinced that the political activities and attitudes of Fr Michael Lapsley constitute a threat to the life of this Province...

Repeatedly, Michael was told by everyone that he needed to follow Trevor Huddleston's example: Huddleston was obedient to the wishes of his Order, the Community of the Resurrection. Huddleston suddenly became an example to follow, not in his overt identification with the ANC, but in his compliance with the wishes of his Religious Order. To be sure, the two cases had some similarity, but also many differences: Huddleston was, after all, in South Africa at the time; Michael was in an independent African country, Lesotho. Huddleston would almost certainly have been arrested along with the other Treason Trialists.[39] Nevertheless, even in the most conservative interpretation of "obedience," Huddleston would not have agreed that it was simply a matter of obeying commands from the ecclesiastical "on high." The more enlightened position and certainly the more positive, some thirty years later, is that "obedience," in large measure, has much more to do with finding the will of God and analyzing the dictates of conscience, than obeying blindly the will of particular people in authority.

---

[39] See Worsnip, *Between the two fires*, 114.

❦CHAPTER 4

Here we go again?

The question of obedience: this issue was to become key during Michael's stay in Zimbabwe. Indeed, it has always been an issue, and perhaps always will be. One thing is very clear: Michael's commitment to the Religious life has been very much stronger than the commitment of some of his brothers to him; and this seems to me to be rather tragic.

For someone outside the family of those who commit themselves to this particular kind of living and these ideals, I have always found it difficult to understand what the "pull" is — clearly, there is the security. Even though Religious are committed (in some respect, at least) to vows of poverty, chastity and obedience, it remains in some ways, easier to live out the Christian life as a Religious than as a "secular" person, or priest, or anything else for that matter. Indeed, are the terms themselves not faintly ridiculous? What does it mean to be a "Religious"? What does it mean to be "secular"? Although Religious are committed to poverty, it usually is a very strange kind of poverty: it means never having to worry ever again about where one's next meal is coming from, taxes or the price of houses or cars, or any of the things to which "secular" people devote an extra-ordinary amount of time and energy; it means that you will live for the rest of your days in relative comfort (not luxury certainly), but comfort nonetheless. Many a calling to the Religious life is based on precisely that sort of consideration, although perhaps not overtly or even consciously. However, if one honestly considers a country like Lesotho, the chances of poverty, or dire squalor, or worse, are very high. Not even the people with education have jobs. Why not say a few Offices a day for the price of a warm bed and three meals? Perhaps in Europe or North America, where real poverty is not quite the issue it is here (although perhaps it is even there), there might be more "spiritual" motives. Of course, there are other motives here, too.

Running away from sexuality of one sort or another is often a strong motivation. Very few Religious are asexual, I would imagine. Many may have problematic sexualities which the nunnery or monastery hopefully would, if not solve, then at least mask, or at least allow one not to deal with. Chastity is seldom the issue, sexuality frequently is. A good friend of mine, a Religious, once said to me, "When I became a Religious, I took three vows, Poverty, Chastity, and Obedience. Well," he said with a glint in his eye, "two out of three isn't bad!" Honestly, I never really did work out which of the last two was the problem for him — I had my suspicions, naturally, and I'm sure that that was what was intended.

When Michael was four years old, he remembers announcing to his brother, Peter, that when he grew up, he wanted either to be a priest or a clown. On the day of his ordination, he received a message from his brother saying, "Now you have achieved both."

When the members of Michael's Religious Order treated him so badly, very naturally there was the thought of withdrawing. It was certainly something which came very easily to my mind, but for Michael, it was never, and could never be, a very likely possibility. I remember talking through the issue with Michael late into one night in 1983, when by chance we had landed in Manchester together. I urged him to leave: what was the Order doing for him? How could he tolerate the kind of treatment he was receiving from them? I remember the real turmoil, the agony on Michael's face. The SSM was his family, how could he leave them? Even though many of them were prepared to vilify him, denounce him, and in the end, deny him, he could not give them up. He just could not, and one just had to leave it at that.

Michael angers people — perhaps less so now than he did then. He angers people because he speaks a message they do not want to hear; this includes his own brethren. In some quarters of the Society, the support has been extremely strong, not least from successive Directors. However, in the Southern African Province, the support has been weak and often lacking completely; occasionally members of the Society have been actively, and sometimes almost obsessively, opposed to Michael, his message, his gospel, his politics, his views, everything. With such rejection, there has been considerable pain, and the people who inflict it do not see it, or choose not to see it; rather, they would have agreed with Bishop Donald Nestor, that Michael was in fact, hurting himself. They were wrong.

Michael left Lesotho and went to Britain to consult with the Director of SSM, Father Edmund Wheat. Michael set up with one of the brethren who lives a rather eccentric and solitary life in Longsight, a suburb of Manchester. While waiting for the outcome of his appeal, Michael used the opportunity to travel widely, speaking about South Africa. Fr Edmund had written to Michael in Lesotho expressing a totally different interpretation of the issue of obedience from the one which was being thrown in his face by others. He wrote to Michael: "All I can do is assure you of my thoughts and prayers at this time and express the hope that you will think carefully about any advice people will offer you and act according to your conscience."[1]

While Michael was in Manchester, the Society was very much aware that his time would be used to contribute to the cause of the struggle of the people of South Africa, and that Michael's contribution would be within a context of a very specific commitment to the ANC.[2]

The CPSA immediately (and perhaps with sighs of relief) assumed that Michael had finally agreed to "further his studies" in Manchester, and the Executive Officer wrote to Michael, responding yet again on the Archbishop's behalf, repeating that there had been no outcome to the appeal, and wishing Michael well with his studies.[3] Michael was not amused and responded immediately saying that far from being involved in studies, he was "anxiously awaiting the outcome of my appeal in the prayerful hope that I will soon be able to return to continue working in the Diocese of Lesotho."[4]

The appeal failed, as we have seen, and Michael prepared to make the kind of change which few of us find easy. True, he was a Religious, and Religious are supposed to be able to uproot and leave

---

[1] Fr Edmund Wheat, SSM, letter to Michael Lapsley, January 8, 1983.

[2] Michael Lapsley, interview, Pietermaritzburg, July 5, 1992.

[3] The Rt Revd F. Amoore, letter to Michael Lapsley, June 22, 1983.

[4] Michael Lapsley, letter to The Most Revd P. Russell, July 7, 1983. While Michael was in Britain, he met with Bishop Mokuku, the Diocesan Bishop of Lesotho, who was on sabbatical in Britain at the time. The Bishop indicated that he was willing to reverse the decision and allow Michael to return to the Diocese by the end of the year. However, on the Bishop's return from sabbatical, it was the Provincial of SSM, Fr Clement Mullinger, who made it quite impossible for the Bishop to reverse the decision. Michael Lapsley, interview, July 5, 1992.

at a moment's notice; they should not be bound to places, or people, or things — for the sake of the gospel.

For the sake of the gospel they should be prepared to leave everything behind and start afresh, anywhere. They should be able to do this, because of obedience. I know Michael too well to believe for a single moment that this was an easy move. I remember very clearly the look of pain which came over his eyes when we spoke, some time later in Zimbabwe, about the new warden to the students at Lelapa la Jesu Seminary in Lesotho. "I'm finding it difficult to talk about that," he said, and we said no more for a while.

Fr Edmund Wheat SSM is almost your archetypal image of a monk: he is large, yet delicate; slightly (ever so slightly) epicene; he has a balding, rounded head with squarish spectacles squeezed there-on, which leave marks on his head when he takes them off and leave you startled because he looks so unfamiliar without them. He has an extremely sharp wit, a delightful twinkle in his eye, a framed picture of a lifesized Holland's steak and kidney pie on his desk, and both a humanity and a fairness which makes one stop and stare.

Edmund loves food passionately. "When I became a monk," he announced in a rather swish Manchester restaurant once, "I substituted food for sex."

"Oh yes!" he reassures his listener, wide-eyed and insistent after the laughter, "it's absolutely true!" as he throws another forkfull of whatever it is he is enjoying elegantly into his mouth.

Edmund understood obedience in a way that many others did not. For him, obedience was not a matter of simply obeying what the hierarchy wanted; in fact nothing could be further from its meaning. Obedience meant being obedient to the will of God and the dictates of conscience, and it could well be the case that obedience to the will of God and the following of the dictates of conscience would conflict with what others wanted for one.

Michael, in consultation with the Society, had decided to enroll at the University of Zimbabwe under Professor Adrian Hastings, to do a Masters Degree. He also managed to secure for himself a job in the Diocese of Harare. Edmund Wheat had come out to Zimbabwe to discuss the position with the Diocesan Bishop, Peter Hatendi. He wrote a covering letter to Michael, enclosing a copy of the letter to the Bishop:

> Greetings from England! And many thanks for your kindness during my visit to Harare. It was most enjoyable.

That cannot be said for the flight which I found a bit claustrophobic as well as not giving me ample room to stretch out. However, I sat next to a nice family. The man was Secretary of some Evangelical Missionary Society — but obviously quite liberal in some ways. The Bp of Matabeleland was also on board and we had some fellowship at Kilimanjaro![5]

His letter to the Bishop is important because of what transpired later.

...I am also writing to confirm the decisions that were made about Fr Michael's future in Zimbabwe. As I understand it, he will be given a contract by the Diocese of Harare for three years and be employed at the Cathedral in the first instance and then hopefully in one of the high density area parishes. I am happy with this arrangement and I hope that Michael will be happy too to serve the Church in your Diocese.[6]

Two memoranda from Diocesan Secretary, I.M. Maspero were drawn up, the first stating that Michael was to assume office as rector of Mbare with effect from August 1, 1985, and working out salary scales;[7] the second asking the Bishop whether he was ready to sign the contract for Michael's appointment since there had been a delay caused by the Chief Immigration Officer.[8] Clearly, Michael seemed set to be appointed to the position of rector of the parish of St Michael's, Mbare.

Mbare was one of the first "township" areas of what was then Salisbury, Rhodesia. It is poor, crowded, dusty and unattractive in almost all respects. The parish church of St Michael's was, in fact, or was seen as the "black" cathedral of Salisbury, given the inherent racism of the "white" cathedral in town. It is a very large church, once boasting a very large congregation; but of late, it had become a rather sad and directionless parish. When Michael came to the parish, he waved no magic wand, but he did insist on democratic decision-making, and succeeded in fanning the wan flame of the congregation

---

[5] Fr E. Wheat SSM, letter to Michael Lapsley, December 20, 1984.

[6] Fr E. Wheat SSM, letter to The Rt Revd P. Hatendi, December 20, 1984.

[7] I.M. Maspero, memorandum to Fr Lapsley, July 15, 1985.

[8] I.M. Maspero, memorandum to the Bishop of Harare, August 14, 1985.

Michael Lapsley's house
(left) after the bombing
Photo: The Herald/Sunday Mail

Michael Lapsley (below)
in hospital in Australia,
June 1990

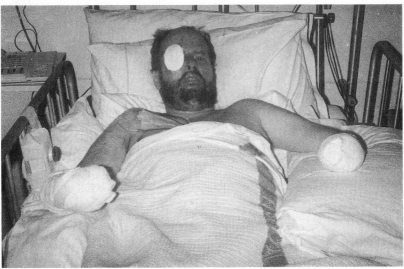

Michael as a young child

Michael with his two brothers

Michael Lapsley as a young priest, July 1971, Australia

Fr Trevor Huddleston in
Sophiatown on the day of
the forced removals, 1953
Photo: IDAF

Archbishop Trevor
Huddleston at his 80th
birthday mass giving the
ANC salute

Michael Lapsley with
Archbishop Huddleston in
Johannesburg

Michael Lapsley with Oliver Tambo, National Chairperson of the ANC, November 1992, Johannesburg

Michael Lapsley with President Nelson Mandela at the Cuba Solidarity Conference, Johannesburg, October 1995

Michael Lapsley leading an anti-apartheid protest march in Harare, Zimbabwe, 1987
Photo: The Herald

Then President of Zimbabwe, Canaan Banana, and his wife with Michael Lapsley
in St Michael's Parish Church, Mbare, Harare, 1986. Photo: The Herald/Sunday Mail

Black Sash protest, Pietermaritzburg, May 1990

Michael Lapsley with parishioners at St Michael's Parish Church, Mbare, Harare, July 19, 1986 Photo: The Herald/Sunday Mail

Michael Lapsley (right)
Photo: Lars Pehrson

Michael Lapsley (below)
with his sisters
Helen and Irene in London,
November 1995

Michael Lapsley with children, North Bay, Canada, November 1991

into something of a blaze. One St Michael's parishioner of 20 years' standing said that he had never seen such a good "turn up" of the congregation as was the case since Michael's arrival.[9] Michael thrived in this situation of a"township" parish with "township" life and "township" issues — a "township" not terribly different from the hundreds and thousands in South Africa. It was a place where Michael could feel at home and at one, somewhere he could feel as though the work he was doing was worth something and was making a difference. Michael knew he would be happy in such a place.

Imagine his shock several months after his appointment to St Michael's to read in the *Diocesan Prayer Calendar* for January 1986, his name mentioned (together with that of Fr John Weller), as warden of the soon-to-be-established Gaul House — a theological college which was being set up in the Diocese.

In January 1986 the churchwardens of St Michael's received a letter from Bishop Hatendi[10] wherein the Bishop indicated his decision to move Michael from the parish to the Wardenship of Gaul House. The churchwardens immediately wrote to the Bishop stating that they felt it would be "in the interests of St Michael's and the Diocese" that Michael should remain rector of St Michael's parish. "The tributaries must flow, if the big river is to exist." "This may appear to be a rude and selfish answer to your letter my Lord, but truth sometimes tend (sic) to be stubborn," they argued and offered the Bishop the following reasons why Michael should not be moved:

1. We have deliberately put the parish in debt by carrying out hall roof repairs and painting with the full faith that that with the current motivation we would get through by June.
2. The attendance is picking up very well that we have the full hope that with Fr Lapsley as rector, we will be in a position to call ourselves a true parish before the end of the year.
3. The youth are beginning to be organized and participate in the parish.

---

[9] Minutes of an emergency meeting, St Michael's, Mbare, Parish Hall, March 16, 1986.

[10] The Rt Revd P. Hatendi, letter to the churchwardens of St Michael's Parish Mbare, January 15, 1986.

4. A new fire has been kindled and it is only fair that it is kept burning.[11]

Irritated, Michael also wrote to the Bishop. He did, however, take the precaution of reading the letter to a senior priest in the Diocese:

I appreciate your confidence in me as a possible warden of Ordinands and also the dilemma facing you in the Diocese... I think it fair that I convey to you at the earliest opportunity my own response to your overtures.

It was agreed by the Director of SSM and myself that I would accept your invitation to become the rector of St Michael's Parish after three months at the Cathedral. The churchwardens, Church Council and Parishioners at St Michael's were all informed that I was coming to be the parish priest and certainly not a "pro-tem" arrangement...

When I arrived at St Michael's, I found a parish with a rich past, but also a parish which was losing ground and had lost confidence in itself. With God's help, I believe that we are beginning to build a strong Christian community at St Michael's. This building is beginning to take shape but is at a delicate and fragile stage.

I think that it would not be fair to the people of this parish for me to leave here at this time. I think it is fair that I make it clear that I would not be able to accede to an offer at this stage to take over the wardenship full-time at Gaul House.[12]

It was at this stage, Michael suggests, that "something snapped inside the Bishop's brain."[13] Indeed, the Bishop was not pleased. He declared that Michael and the churchwardens were wrong in all of seven respects: [I paraphrase]

1. Assumption — the assumption that the Bishop (sic) does not know the needs of the parish of St Michael's. It was he who chaired the Vestry meeting in which the church-wardens were elected and he who offered Michael the parish.

---

[11] L. Matiza and A.C.C. Pasipanodya, letter to The Rt Revd P Hatendi, January 20, 1986.

[12] Michael Lapsley, letter to The Rt Revd P. Hatendi, January 23, 1986.

[13] Lapsley, interview, July 5, 1992.

2. Transfer — all full-time priests are transferable at short notice. Contrary to what Michael thought, he was not being transferred from St Michael's parish, but from the Cathedral, since he was not yet licensed to serve as parish priest at St Michael's.

3. Consultation — Transfers are made between the Bishop and the priest concerned, or the Bishop and the churchwardens or between the Bishop and the Archdeacon in Senate. Since the churchwardens had shown Michael the letter they received from the Bishop, a "breach of confidence" had occurred setting Michael and the churchwardens against the Bishop and Senate.

4. Authority — authority to transfer is not given to the Bishop in Senate by the churchwardens or the Director of SSM because this would have the effect of setting aside Michael's canonical oath of obedience to the Bishop. The Diocese is Michael's employer, not the Parish of St Michael's.

5. License — It is the Diocesan Bishop who gives a priest a license, not the churchwardens.

6. Needs — Only the Bishop knows the overall needs of the Diocese which "he tries to satisfy through the staff at his command." Gaul House is for the good of the whole Diocese, St Michael's parish included. "A parochial spirit should not be encouraged...."

7. Danger — "the danger of the move you and the churchwardens have taken is obvious. It is divisive to say the least and makes me wonder."[14]

It is a very odd letter. Edmund Wheat, who received a similar letter to this one, described it as, "Completely legalistic with no attempt to see it from a personal or pastoral point of view. Slightly pathological I thought... I don't envy him his job but he must learn to treat people like people or he will be up shit's creek. I replied as nicely as I could but felt that I just couldn't be walked over."[15]

The churchwardens went to see the Bishop to appeal directly to him on behalf of the congregation. After what was termed a "long discussion," the Bishop finally relented and told the churchwardens

---

[14] The Rt Revd P. Hatendi, letter to Michael Lapsley, January 27, 1986.

[15] Fr E. Wheat SSM, letter to Michael Lapsley, February 24, 1986.

to "go and tell the people that Fr Michael was to stay."[16] A date for his induction was set. The Bishop wrote to Michael three days later apologizing for not having offered him the post of warden of Gaul House in writing.[17] Edmund Wheat wrote to Michael from Britain saying that he was sure that he had been right to say no to the college post: "I think it would be unfair on the parish and I feel your present work is right for you at the moment." He commented that he felt that Michael had had enough of running "tin-pot seminaries."[18]

The Bishop then wrote to Michael again admitting that he had not consulted him over the wardenship of Gaul House:

> I had wrongly assumed that all stipendiary clergymen in this Diocese including me have voluntarily surrendered all their priestly time to serving God and were under orders to transfer with or without notice. The will of God is known in the Diocese through synods and standing committee which... charged me on the understanding that the Diocesan staff will, in turn, take orders from me.[19]

The Bishop then went on to state, under the heading "airfare," that the Diocese would be responsible for Michael's air ticket to the UK "as a token of our appreciation of your tremendous contribution to this Diocese." The letter ended with the heading "Tribute": "You are doing a good job at Mbare for which we are sincerely grateful and we shall miss you very much."[20]

On March 16, the churchwardens asked the Bishop to come to explain to the congregation why he had made the decision to "banish" Fr Michael to England. The meeting was a stormy one. The Bishop came accompanied by his wife and the Archdeacon of Harare, The Venerable S. Bakare. The minutes of the meeting are extremely revealing:

---

[16] A.C.C. Pasipanodya and L. Matiza, memorandum, "Rev Michael Lapsley. St Michael's Parish Mbare — rector designate."
[17] The Rt Revd P. Hatendi, letter to Michael Lapsley, January 31, 1986.
[18] Fr E. Wheat SSM, letter to Michael Lapsley, January 31, 1986, also Michael Lapsley, interview, July 5, 1992.
[19] The Rt Revd P. Hatendi, letter to Michael Lapsley, March 9, 1986.
[20] Ibid.

The Bishop showed the members the *Acts of the Diocese.* He explained briefly the purpose of the Acts and said they [were] used in [the] administration of the Diocese and to ensure its smooth running. The Acts were passed by Synod. Any changes or alterations of the Acts would have to pass at Synod. The Bishop therefore had to act in accordance with the Acts....

According to the Acts, the Bishop had found that Fr Michael had breached certain rules.

He had refused to be sent.

He had broken the oath of obedience.[21]

When the parishioners finally got to speak, they expressed their unanimous desire to be allowed to keep Michael as their priest. The Bishop, however, was adamant. Michael had broken canonical obedience and must be removed. The parishioners were angry and accused the Bishop alternately of trying to make himself infallible, of being a rumormonger and of being influenced by his wife, later remarking, "We do not know why she was brought to this meeting, unless she had become the uncrowned assistant Bishop of Harare."[22]

The parish had erupted into a virtual volcano of discontent. The Bishop suspected that Michael had in fact orchestrated the whole thing, writing to Michael: "When we met on Friday you forewarned me that the parish is mobilized against my decision and that the parish will fall apart if I do not yield to their demands. You were quite right; but how did you know?"[23]

The Bishop wrote his own "Amendments and corrections to the minutes of the emergency meeting" held at St Michael's Parish on March 16.[24] The Bishop argues in this document that the word "transfer" used with regard to Michael is misleading.

---

[21] Minutes of an emergency meeting, March 16, 1986.

[22] A.C.C. Pasipanodya and L. Matiza, memorandum, "Rev Michael Lapsley. St Michael's Parish Mbare — rector designate."

[23] The Rt Revd P. Hatendi, letter to Michael Lapsley, March 16, 1986.

[24] The Rt Revd P. Hatendi, "Amendments and corrections to the minutes of the emergency meeting of St Michael's Parish Representatives held on Passion Sunday March 16, 1986 at St Michael's Parish Hall with the Bishop in the Chair."

Fr Michael has not yet been employed. What the Bishop wanted to do, if Fr Michael had agreed, was to appoint him to the wardenship of Gaul House, as he wanted to appoint/induct him to the incumbency of St Michael's Parish last year. Fr Michael is holding the fort on behalf of the Bishop at St Michael's Parish. He is not the official incumbent at St Michael's Parish. To turn down an appointment is to refuse to be employed. This is what Fr Michael did. When a priest/messenger is employed he can turn down the Bishop's transfer notice; but he must start by accepting the transfer. "Yes, I shall go, but..." This is acceptable... The Bishop listens to reasons for and against a transfer. Priests, like policemen are messengers in a missionary Diocese (sic?). Although Fr Michael has signed the contract of service the Bishop has not yet signed his part on behalf of the Diocese. He will not sign it on behalf of a parish.[25]

After the Sunday meeting, the Bishop called an emergency meeting of the Senate in order decide what to do. "In my limited experience as a Bishop of this Diocese I have not chaired such a meeting when threats were hailed (sic) at me. It was an eyeopener," he wrote to Michael.[26]

What the Bishop found hard to take and understand was the heckling and intimidation as well as the insults hailed (sic) at his wife. Christians do not behave like this and if this has anything to do with you the Bishop has a problem on his hands.[27]

The Bishop also called upon Michael to "withdraw publicly... and in writing" what he had said in the meeting about the authority of the *Constitution and Canons* and the *Acts of the Diocese of Harare*.

According to the minutes of the meeting[28] the Bishop had brought along with him a copy of the *Acts of the Diocese of Harare* and explained to the meeting what their purpose was and the fact

---

[25] Ibid.
[26] The Rt Revd P Hatendi, letter to Michael Lapsley, March 16, 1986.
[27] The Rt Revd P. Hatendi, letter to Michael Lapsley, March 20, 1986.
[28] Minutes of an emergency meeting, March 16, 1986.

that he had to act in accordance with those Acts.[29] Michael then took a copy of the Bible together with the copy of the Acts of the Diocese of Harare and contended that the Acts gave a legal framework which was "very important for the Church as an institution, [in the same way as]... any institution should have a legal framework."[30] The Bible, however, was a book about relationships between God and people and between people and people. He suggested that in terms of the *Acts of the Diocese*, neither the parish, nor he had any power. To refer to the Acts in this situation was therefore fruitless, because the problem was essentially one of relationships. He said that he believed that if he were forced to leave St Michael's at this time, the Diocese, the parish, and he himself would be the losers. All that would be proved was that the Bishop had the power to remove him.[31] The Bishop could not agree with this, responding:

> The issue is not one of power but of conscience. The Bishop has no more power than you and the parish have because we are members of one body. When employing a priest the Bishop does it on behalf of the Diocese and assumes a collective conscience on the strength of the information before him. Ultimately the parish accepts the decision of the Bishop. Of the three books, the Bible has the last say.[32] What the parish may not do is to dictate to the Bishop as it did on Sunday because a priest is appointed to the service of the Diocese and not to the service of a parish. The Bishop and parishes are one.[33]

The issue dragged on and on; the churchwardens made written and oral representations to the Senate; which in turn referred the matter to the Bishop. The Bishop wrote legalistic letters to the churchwardens demanding "three or two... licensed clergymen resident in

---

[29] Ibid.

[30] Ibid.

[31] Ibid., Michael confirms what was said in the letter which he wrote to the Bishop on the matter see Michael Lapsley, letter to The Rt Revd P Hatendi, March 19, 1986.

[32] Bishop Hatendi had pointed out that there were, in fact, three books in question, the other was the *Constitution and Canons*. See The Rt Revd P. Hatendi, letter to Michael Lapsley, March 20, 1986.

[33] Ibid.

this Diocese to submit written references to the Bishop in confidence...." [34] In the meantime, Michael received a letter from the Bishop dismissing him from the post of Examining Chaplain on the ground that Michael and the Bishop had "disagreed on several clauses relating to [his]... contract"[35] Michael was also asked to resign from all committees which had anything to do with the theological college.[36]

Michael had been, up to this time, chairperson of both the Diocesan and National Theological Commissions. The Church-wardens again wrote to the Bishop making the same request, this time with the unanimous backing of both the parish Council and the congregation of St Michael's.[37] The Bishop again replied, this time saying that the churchwardens were "forcing the Bishop to break his oath of canonical obedience made at his consecration."

"I would rather resign," he wrote, "than break the oath which I made before the face of God and in the presence of the Cathedral congregation as witnesses."[38]

The Bishop then offered a compromise for Michael to consider, that his application for appointment and the nomination of the churchwardens would only be considered if it was unconditional.

The nub of the matter, in fact, was that the Bishop was under the impression that obedience meant being willing to do whatever God, through the Bishop, decided. This in reality meant doing what the Bishop decided — agree first, then discuss. The Bishop interpreted the issue of obedience in such a way that because Michael was a Religious he should be twice as obedient as a secular priest. In fact, this issue of obedience looked more like an issue of power. In itself it presents a very interesting situation: Religious do not depend on bishops for their livelihood, secular priests do. That subtle difference means that very often secular priests are prepared to put up with a great deal of pushing and shoving and blind militaristic demands for

---

[34] See A.C.C. Pasipanodya and L. Matiza, letter to The Ven. S. Bakare, March 25, 1986, and The Rt Revd P. Hatendi, letter to the churchwardens, March 27, 1986.

[35] The Rt Revd P. Hatendi, letter to Michael Lapsley, April 9, 1986.

[36] Ibid.

[37] A.C.C. Pasipanodya and L. Matiza, letter to The Rt Revd P. Hatendi, April 15, 1986.

[38] The Rt Revd P. Hatendi, letter to the churchwardens, April 15, 1986.

obedience, Religious or not, because in the end the Bishop controls the purse strings. Not to put too fine a point on it — that is power.

Had Michael been a normal secular priest in Zimbabwe in such circumstances, he would simply have lost his job, or possibly come back in a few years seeking forgiveness and been reinstated according to the whim of the Bishop. Had he been a normal expatriate priest, he would simply have been sent home. Because Michael was a Religious, he had other options and that was clearly a tremendous threat to the Bishop.

Bishop Hatendi admitted to Michael, at a meeting a few months later on May 7, that the only reason he had for moving Michael was to "prove obedience."[39] This issue of obedience was once again evident when the Bishop returned to Harare from a visit to Jerusalem to discover that Michael had organized an Africa Day celebration in the parish hall, attended by over one thousand people, including diplomats and various party officials inside and outside the country, as well as the Anglican Bishop of Namibia. The Bishop observed that this meeting "must have taken lots of planning and preparation," and therefore wanted to know: "Who convened the meeting? Who gave permission for the church hall to be used? Why did you not inform me, the Vicar-General in my absence or the Archdeacon? I am sure you must have informed the police."[40]

At the same time, the Bishop had called a Vestry meeting.[41] The meeting is usually called by the parish priest, but in the bishop's interpretation, seeing no parish priest had been appointed by him, he called the meeting himself. However, the congregation boycotted the meeting, demanding instead to know about Michael's future in the Diocese of Harare. Naturally, the Bishop again assumed that Michael was behind the boycott and demanded that he "prove beyond reasonable doubt" that he knew nothing about it and that he was "as surprised as the Vicar-General and the Archdeacon were at this form of blackmail."[42]

The Bishop saw a connection between the "defiance of authority" related to the arranging of the Africa Day Service and the cancell-

---

[39] Michael Lapsley, letter to The Rt Revd P. Hatendi, May 12, 1986.

[40] The Rt Revd P. Hatendi, letter to Michael Lapsley, June 3, 1986.

[41] Vestry meetings, usually held annually, are the way in which Anglican churches function at a parish level. It is at the Vestry Meeting that the parish council is elected and thus, the parish is governed.

[42] Ibid.

ation of the annual Vestry meeting. The issue, it seemed, was not so much that Africa Day was celebrated, but rather that because it was so important an occasion, in view of the many dignitaries who had been invited, why was the Bishop (or his representative) not invited. The Bishop of Namibia happened to be in Harare in transit at the time, and happily accepted an invitation to the celebration, given on the spur of the moment. God forbid he should have been formally invited to the service without the Bishop of Harare's knowledge! Apparently Bishops are very protective over who does what in their dioceses. So protective, in fact, that the Bishop of Harare actually phoned the Bishop of Namibia, "at 1650 hours local time" to find out if he had been invited formally to come specially from Namibia, or not. The Bishop of Namibia explained that he "was in Harare on the day in question. I would have attended a church service anywhere in Harare; but I went to St Michael's Parish Church at the rector's invitation."[43]

Obviously, the issue here is power. It is a very sad thing to behold, when a first generation black leadership starts behaving with the same kind of crudity (and even worse) as did the previous white racist leadership of the same church.

Michael was subsequently told that he was "free to quit the rectory" during the month of July.[44] The Archdeacon of Harare West, the churchwardens and the Diocesan Secretary were all informed that Michael "will quit the rectory... during the month of July."[45] Michael could not understand why, if he was still employed by the Diocese, and not having yet been dismissed, he was now being told that he was "free to quit the rectory."[46]

It seems this was the final straw; the Bishop wrote informing Michael that his license to administer the sacraments in the Diocese would expire at the end of the month. The Bishop also offered to pay for a single air ticket for him to South Africa (of all places), the United Kingdom or New Zealand.[47] The cynicism of the offer of an air ticket to South Africa for a known member of the ANC in 1986,

---

[43] The Rt Revd P. Hatendi, letter to Michael Lapsley, June 11, 1986.

[44] The Rt Revd P. Hatendi, letter to Michael Lapsley, June 25, 1986.

[45] The Rt Revd P. Hatendi, memorandum to the Archdeacon of Harare West, churchwardens of St Michael's Parish and the Diocesan Secretary, June 25, 1986.

[46] Michael Lapsley, letter to The Rt Revd P. Hatendi, July 2, 1986.

[47] The Rt Revd P. Hatendi, letter to Michael Lapsley, July 2, 1986, and The Rt Revd P. Hatendi, letter to Michael Lapsley, July 4, 1986.

is extremely difficult to indulge — even from someone in as irrational a state as appears to be the case.

The Bishop started receiving anonymous letters about his decision to move Michael, and as usual assumed that Michael was behind them, and wrote to him:

> The... mail brought this anonymous aerogramme from, your loyal followers: WABVISA FR MIKE! NEWE UCHABVAWO! WHAT KIND OF BISHOP! DACHYA RABISHPOP! MUNHU AKABARWA! CHASARA KUFA! KANA URI MUNO CHASARA! KUENDA FANIKA ZVA! WAITA FR MIKE! GO AND SLEEP WITH YOUR WIFE!
>
> For your information my name at birth is "CHABARWA CHINYI CHICHAFA." I shall die before them; but they will follow me one by one. I am ready to die for my decision; but please spare my wife. She did not influence my decision....
>
> I offered you the whole Diocese save Mbare and you refused. Why Mbare? You owe me an explanation and not vice versa... Demonstrating against my decision is not in our mutual interests; but there is nothing I can do to stop the demonstration and the publicity. The decision is yours.[48]

Eventually Michael issued the following statement:

> In January 1986, Bishop Hatendi informed the other bishops in Zimbabwe and the churchwardens of St Michael's, Mbare, that I was to go and run a new seminary in Mt Pleasant. I felt that it would not be right to go there on a full-time basis when I had only been at Mbare six months and had not come on a temporary basis to Mbare. The parish also earnestly requested the Bishop to allow me to stay at St Michael's whilst assisting with the seminary. The Bishop had told others that I would be going to run the seminary without consulting me. The Bishop wrote to apologize that he had never offered me the job in Mt Pleasant.
>
> Initially the Bishop said I could stay in Mbare but then changed his mind. For six months the parish has been trying to persuade the Bishop that I should stay, but he has

---

[48] The Rt Revd P. Hatendi, letter to Michael Lapsley, July 8, 1986.

steadfastly refused. The Bishop says that I must leave to prove obedience and also because he cannot give in to the will of the people. The Bishop has said that the people are following me and not Jesus. He has also accused the people of being dissidents.

Whilst I have asked to stay at St Michael's, I have not refused to leave or be transferred. The people feel that they should have a say in whether a priest goes or stays. If they are happy with him, he should not be transferred or dismissed without good reason.

On July 4, the Bishop wrote to say that I was being dismissed as from July 31. I received another letter on July 14 to say that I was dismissed as from July 19 and must leave the house before that date.

The contract I signed when I came to work for the Diocese provides for six months' notice by either party. I was left with no alternative but to go to the Ministry of Labor to obtain the elementary justice and compassion which I was being denied by the Church.

I was recruited by the Diocese of Harare whilst already in Zimbabwe. The Bishop has offered me air tickets to London, New Zealand and South Africa and it appears he has also contacted the Department of Immigration. An impression of attempted deportation has been created.

I am deeply saddened that the Bishop has acted only in pursuit of what he calls "law and order" and with callous disregard for my rights or for the needs and wishes of the people.

It is shameful for the whole Church when a Christian has to appeal to the state to obtain protection from arbitrary eviction and illegal abrogation of contract.

The Bishop has the technical authority to remove my right to take services and administer sacraments. However, my priesthood does not come from any human being but as a call of God. Even if I can no longer offer the Mass, I will try to live it. I will seek with God's help to be a faithful priest and to be true to the liberating gospel of Jesus Christ, who took sides with the poor and downtrodden and led them in the struggle for total liberation.[49]

---

[49] Michael Lapsley, statement, July 20, 1986.

Eventually the whole matter was taken to the Labor Relations Officer and heard at two sittings. It was finally agreed that: "The two parties should part on condition that the Bishop recommends to immigration for Fr Michael's work permit. Father Michael voluntarily decided not to claim any terminal benefits."[50]

A "reconciliation," of sorts, had taken place. The Bishop wrote to "inform" Michael that "as far as we are concerned mutual forgiveness" had taken place.[51] Michael tried on four separate occasions after this to get the return of his license, but to no avail. "That decision stands unconditionally, painful as it is to all concerned," wrote the Bishop.[52] The decision stood, even when Michael's father died and he wrote to the Bishop asking for special dispensation to say a requiem Mass for his father.[53] "I live and work within the Diocese of Harare," wrote Michael, "but I am not able to administer the sacraments within your jurisdiction. I continue to feel excluded and unforgiven."[54] The Bishop did not relent. "...In view of the fact that nothing to our knowledge has changed we regret to inform you that your application was unsuccessful."[55]

Michael decided, with the full blessing of SSM, to continue working in Zimbabwe, with the Lutheran World Federation. Interestingly, he obtained licenses from the other three Anglican bishops of Zimbabwe and was able to function as a priest in their Dioceses. With respect to the Bishop of Harare, however, Michael said that he was the "importunate widow" who would continue knocking until the door was opened.

Soon after the bombing, however, the Bishop came to see Michael in hospital. Jenny Hanekom announced that Bishop Hatendi was there to see him. Michael paused for a moment and then said in a scampish way... "Bishop who?"

On November 12, 1990, while Michael was in Australia, having corrective surgery, he once again wrote to the Bishop asking for his license. The Bishop replied, "It is a miracle that you are still alive and

[50] On November 24, 1986, and December 9, 1986, see "Determination of Matter" between The Diocese of Mashonaland (sic) and Father Lapsley, January 21, 1987.
[51] The Rt Revd P. Hatendi, letter to Michael Lapsley, June 4, 1987.
[52] Ibid.
[53] Michael Lapsley, letter to The Rt Revd P Hatendi, August 4, 1987.
[54] Michael Lapsley, letter to The Rt Revd P. Hatendi, March 25, 1988.
[55] The Rt Revd P. Hatendi, letter to Michael Lapsley, May 31, 1988.

we thank God for his power and love. Please find enclosed a temporary license duly completed and signed."[56]

---

[56] The Rt Revd P. Hatendi, letter to Michael Lapsley, November 12, 1990. The Bishop's own story was to take on even more extraordinary proportions later on, when he refused to stand down as Bishop at the time of reaching retirement age. The story is not a salutary one, and eventually involved Bishop Hatendi virtually being forced from his position by the Archbishop of Central Africa, Walter Makulu. The incident received a great deal of media coverage in Zimbabwe, see for example "Hatendi agrees to retire from Diocese," The *Herald,* June 12, 1995.

❦CHAPTER 5

Neutrality or co-option?

"There is no such animal as neutrality," wrote Canaan Banana in a foreword to Michael's book, *Neutrality or co-option?*[1]

...neutrality at best means deafening silence and indifference, and at worst smiling at and admiring the status quo. I refuse to accept the notion that Jesus assumed the role of honored guest in the theater of human slaughter and misery. He intervened in human affairs and challenged the principalities and powers that denied God's children their right to life and to fundamental human liberties.[2]

These words by the then President of Zimbabwe, provide an apt summary of what is perhaps the starting point of Michael's theology: God is not neutral and the Church of God cannot be neutral. Usually, when it thinks it is being neutral, it is simply sliding into ideological captivity, a captive to reactionary forces.

Neutrality or co-option? began its life as a Masters thesis at the University of Zimbabwe; it was hardhitting, direct and destined not to be enthusiastically welcomed by the many reactionaries within and without the Church fold in Zimbabwe. Indeed, Canaan Banana mused that some would inevitably view the study as an "explosion" and the author as a "mischief-maker" who "dared to tread in the Holy of holies to excavate the 'sacred' confidentials that should belong to the museum of the privileged few..."[3] One senior priest in

---

[1] Michael Lapsley, *Neutrality or co-option? Anglican Church and State from 1964 until the independence of Zimbabwe*, Gweru, Mambo Press, 1986, 7.

[2] C. Banana, foreword to Michael Lapsley, *Neutrality or co-option?*

[3] Ibid.

the Diocese told Michael that he was hated in the Anglican Church in Zimbabwe because of the book, even before it was published.[4]

The book is an historical study of Church-State relations after the Smith government's Unilateral Declaration of Independence (UDI) in 1964, demonstrating how white control of both Church and state was completely entrenched, to the extent that even the most liberal white missionary tended to end up "a captive of racial prejudice."[5] It showed, however, that other options had been taken as well, by those such as Fr Arthur Shearley Cripps and Bishop Kenneth Skelton, who did not allow themselves to be "co-opted by the dominant ideology."[6] These latter examples were, by no means, radicals. They were not Marxist Christians nor theologians of liberation, but they were committed to theology and their theology informed their faith and their action. Ultimately, their faith was biblical and in many respects very traditional, but within the context of a white, racist, ideologically reactionary Rhodesian Church, they appeared to be extremely radical because they were, at every turn, prepared to "demystify" the "shibboleths" which white Rhodesians had erected around themselves. As a whole, the Rhodesian Anglican Church's most consistent response to such issues as the deepening crisis which UDI had caused, the entrenchment of the illegitimate Smith regime, and the escalating war of independence was, according to Michael Lapsley,

> ...constantly [to] call for reconciliation. Unfortunately, the white leaders were expecting black Christians to be personally reconciled to white Christians without addressing the central issues of power, privilege and wealth which remained in white hands.[7]

Obviously, the concerns which Michael exposes and articulates in his book have a wider application than simply Zimbabwe, but are clearly key concerns with regard to the Church in South Africa as well. Michael's contention was that those, such as Bishop Skelton, who refused to be seduced by the prevailing "orthodoxy" of the

---

[4] Michael Lapsley, speech at the launching of *Neutrality or co-option*, National Gallery, August 18, 1986.

[5] C. Banana, Foreword to Michael Lapsley, *Neutrality or co-option?* 7.

[6] Michael Lapsley, *Neutrality or co-option?*, 71

[7] Ibid., 74.

time, were far from being the "loony left," despite being dubbed "Red Skelton" by the radical right.[8] To a considerable degree, the same must be said of Michael himself. Indeed, Michael was clearly trying to articulate his own position by studying that of others in the Zimbabwe context, having constantly battled to "walk the tightrope" of relations with the state himself. In a sense, the issues in South Africa have always been much sharper. In Lesotho and Zimbabwe the issues are far less distinct.

Michael approached the President of Zimbabwe, Canaan Banana, to write the foreword to his book. Was this not hoisting himself on the selfsame petard as those who identified with the Smith regime? Is it not the case that this demonstrable camaraderie and mutual admiration indicated a very clear identification to "one side" as well? For Michael, there were simple differences between the two situations, such as the clear differences between the government in Zimbabwe and the government in Lesotho. There were clear differences between the government of Zimbabwe and the South African government, the former being a legitimate, popularly-elected government. This did not mean that there were no human rights and justice issues there with which the Church needed to deal. Nevertheless, Michael felt that one could enjoy a good relationship with the state without becoming sycophantic or prostituting his principles — or even theology. Indeed, the weekend before Michael began his work in the parish in Mbare, there had been political conflict between people in the township, where people had been chased out of their houses for having the "wrong" political allegiance — a sadly and frighteningly familiar regional theme. Michael decided to take care to refer to the issue directly in his first sermon, considering it significant enough not to be ignored. On another occasion, "The Party" wanted to hold political rallies at the same time as worship services on Sundays; Michael was part of a ministers' fraternal which challenged members of the cabinet on that issue.[9]

Of course, his role as a "foreign priest" also became an issue. It is often argued that someone from the outside should keep silent, or accept the risk of being thrown out. This argument is used, to great effect, by those who in reality support, albeit tacitly, what is happening (or not happening as the case may be). Or else they argue that one must simply "preach the gospel," the effect of this being that

---

[8] Ibid, 14.
[9] Michael Lapsley, interview, July 5, 1992.

a gospel is preached in which justice has no integral part — gospel so unlike the gospel of Jesus that it is barely recognizable as Christian. If we are to be honest, the prevailing and dominant philosophy in the Christian Church today is really nothing other than Plato writ large and with a vengeance — a gospel primarily concerned with the immortal soul, trapped in a body of grimy materialism, longing to be free. It is a gospel of salvation when we die; and a gospel which enables charismatic preachers, often funded by the United States or similar interests, to roam the planet unaffected by the despair, the misery and the degradation of humankind. Perhaps that is unfair; often they are affected, but they see the solution inevitably as an individual solution, whether it be the individual soul or an individual politician. Michael's option for group identification, for throwing in his lot with a movement of the oppressed, runs completely counter to this philosophy.

A letter to the Harare *Herald* took issue with Michael's stance:

> "It's odd, isn't it, the amount of energy we Christians have devoted to opposing communism...," says Fr Lapsley (*Herald*, March 2). It's even more odd that a Christian priest such as he should devote his energy to supporting communism which is not exactly a Christian ideology.
>
> Surely he should either act as a true Christian priest and give himself wholeheartedly to the spreading of the gospel of Christ — or leave the Ministry and go in for politics.
>
> As it is, he is sullying the reputation of the Christian priesthood.[10]

There was nothing new about this kind of outrage. In 1982, two Anglican parishioners from Pretoria were moved to write to various newspapers in an open letter. They were "distressed to learn of an interview with a priest of our Church" broadcast on the English language "propaganda service of Mozambique," which they described as a country "militantly atheistic."[11] The interviewer asked whether Michael, as a member of the ANC would be prepared to engage in "violent struggle." Michael replied:

---

[10] The *Herald*, March 10, 1987.
[11] Mr and Mrs A. H. Cawood, "Is this a priest of good standing?" *The Star*, March 29, 1982. The broadcast had taken place on February 9, 1982.

The day I became a member of the ANC it meant I had commitments to both the kind of society that the ANC is committed to, but also to accept the command of the organization and its methods of achieving justice. So I accept the full implications of being a member of the ANC and the methodology of armed struggle in order to achieve those aims. So the answer is yes.

Mr and Mrs Cawood wanted to know from the Archbishop of Cape Town (then Philip Russell) whether Michael was still a priest in good standing and licensed in the CPSA and whether it is possible for a priest to "consecrate his life to Christ, and the service of the Church, while simultaneously committing himself to a Marxist organization and its methodology of armed struggle and murder?"

> Bearing in mind the Apostle Peter's exhortation to follow Christ's example of suffering rather than threatening, we would respectfully draw your attention to the fact that Our Lord was born into an inherently unjust society dominated by a colonial army of occupation.
> There existed in Israel at the time a movement called the Zealots, which was dedicated to bringing about national liberation through the armed struggle.
> We understand that reliable Christian scholarship holds that Jesus steadfastly refused to identify with this movement, declaring that His servants could not fight for His Kingdom because it was not of this world.
> He chose rather to submit to every ordinance of man for His Father's sake, even to the extent of paying unjust taxes.[12]

The authors of the letter wanted to know what steps the Archbishop intended taking to discipline Michael Lapsley and they also wanted to know how both the Archbishop and the Anglican Church were intending to dissociate themselves from Michael Lapsley's position.

Archbishop Philip Russell responded by affirming that Michael was a licensed priest in the Diocese of Lesotho. He also affirmed that the Anglican Church accepted the legitimacy of the positions held by both those who took up arms on behalf of the government of the country, those who took up arms against the government, as well as

---

[12] Ibid.

those who refused to take up arms at all. He also stated categorically that the Province had no powers to discipline any priest, only the Diocese could do that and then only within very limited categories. Furthermore, the Church as a whole "seldom associates/dissociates itself with the views expressed by any of its members."[13]

Michael was also given an opportunity to respond and in his reply he said that he welcomed the open letter of Mr and Mrs Cawood because "it provides an opportunity for all Anglicans to consider our attitude towards the ANC and the struggle against apartheid."

> As a follower of Jesus I am committed to the values of peace, love and justice. I understand the Christian gospel to be an option for life, but apartheid, like its close relative, nazism, has always been an option for death that has brought nothing but violence, hatred and injustice to the majority of South Africans.[14]

Michael continued by saying that the ANC was not a Marxist organization, but included Christians, Muslims, Hindus as well as communists and athiests among its members.

To be sure, this has always been a major worry, not to say prejudice, amongst some churchpeople. The ANC is, and always has been, full of people who not only attend Church, but are practising and devout believers. Even the names of the most visible down the years would fill several pages: veteran and cherished names such as Sol Plaatje,[15] Albert Luthuli,[16] Z.K.Matthews,[17] John Dube, Z.R. Mahabane, A.B. Xuma, James Calata and Helen Joseph.[18] Was not Oliver Tambo himself, at one time, an ordinand in the Diocese of Johannesburg; and these are only Christian luminaries. Many millions of others have belonged to the ANC and not been famous.

---

[13] The Most Revd P. Russell, reply to the open letter of Mr and Mrs A.H. Cawood, "Distress over ANC priest's radio remarks," in *Seek*, April/May, 1982.

[14] Michael Lapsley, "I am committed to peace," in Ibid.

[15] See B. Willan, *Sol Plaatje. A biography*, Johannesburg, Ravan, 1984.

[16] A. Luthuli, *Let my people go*, London, Fontana, 1962.

[17] See Z.K. Matthews, *Freedom for my people*, Cape Town and Johannesburg, David Philip, 1981.

[18] H. Joseph, *Side by side: The autobiography of Helen Joseph*, London, Zed Press, 1986.

Many other millions have belonged to faiths other than the Christian faith and in all these cases, their commitment to the ANC has been, more often than not, directly related to their faith. So why the "religious uninformed" should be so worried about the preservation of Christianity in a movement which is patently unconcerned and even encouraging of religious commitment, is difficult to tell — unless there is another reason.

Since at least the late 1970's, it was extremely important for the South African regime to present itself as the paragon of Christian virtue and the ANC and its allies as the devil called Communism. This strategy of dividing the world into two halves was not, by any means, unique to South Africa. It was part of that sinister strategy of Low Intensity Conflict, largely invented because of the thrashing the United States received in Vietnam.[19]

The term "Low Intensity Conflict" (LIC) is a misleading one, as it does not mean that the level of bloodshed or loss of life is low. In Guatemala, for instance, LIC claimed well over 100,000 lives, and similar numbers perished in LIC conflicts elsewhere.[20] Nor does it imply that the war being waged is not devastating in its effects. Rather, the term is used to describe a mode of "irregular" or "unconventional" warfare where troop deployment is kept to a minimum, substituted by the use of surrogate forces, such as the Contras of Nicaragua, the MNR in Mozambique, UNITA in Angola, or the "death squads," train and taxi murderers and other "vigilante" forces in South Africa. On the broad spectrum of conflict, LIC is fought with relatively less actual firepower than in a conventional war, but what is crucial to recognize is that LIC is a type of warfare in which your side suffers very little death or destruction, while the other side suffers as much damage as possible, in a way which produces as little hardship for *your own* society as is practically possible. The most significant feature of this type of warfare is its totality. It involves political, economic and psychological operations in addition to military warfare. The concept of

---

[19] S. Miles, "The real war. Low intensity conflict in Central America," in *Report on the Americas (NACLA Report)*, Vol. XX, No.2 April/May 1986, 20f., The strategy of Low Intensity Conflict continued to be studied, and even more importantly, implemented by the De Klerk regime, despite denials to the contrary and only now are the details becoming known.

[20] M. Klare, "Low Intensity Conflict. The war of the 'haves' against the 'have nots'," in *Christianity and Crisis*, February 1, 1988, 12

LIC has been described as "total war at the grassroots," a war in which "the military is a distant fourth in many cases" — to political, economic and psychological operations.[21]

The South African version of LIC was first implemented under the Botha regime according to the strategic thinking of a little known French military general, Andre Beaufre.[22] Beaufre's thesis is extremely, diabolically, simple. Strategy, he asserts, is always "the art of applying force so that it makes the most effective contribution towards achieving the ends set by political policy."[23]

All forms of strategy, both in terms of warfare and social conflict, can be reduced to what he describes as "a dialectic of wills [where] a decision is achieved when a certain psychological effect has been produced on the enemy: When he becomes convinced that it is useless to start or alternatively to continue the struggle."[24]

The fundamental emphasis, in Beaufre's opinion, needs to be placed on the *psychological surrender* of the enemy as a necessary precondition to its material defeat. This priority must be complemented with an emphasis on war as being perceived as an inevitably "total" phenomenon in the modern age. "Total onslaught" thus demands *total counter-strategy* in order effectively to overcome "the enemy," and this involves a coordinated and aligned military policy with political, financial, economic and also production policies. Military activity is therefore only a single component of a much wider "total" coordination of resources.

---

[21] The *Guardian*, March 12, 1986. See also Colonel J. Waghelstein, "Post Vietnam counterinsurgency doctrine," in *Military Review*, January 1985, 42

[22] See A. Beaufre, *Introduction to Strategy — with particular reference to problems of defense, politics, economics and diplomacy in the nuclear age*, London, Faber and Faber, 1963; for analysis of this see J. Selfe, *The total onslaught and the total strategy. Adaptations to the security intelligence decision-making structures under P.W. Botha's Administration*, unpublished M.A. thesis, University of Cape Town, 1987. See also K.W. Grundy, *The rise of the South African security establishment. An essay on the changing locus of state power*, Johannesburg South African Institute of International Affairs, 1983; and K.W. Grundy, *The militarization of South African politics*, Oxford University Press, 1988. See also for an up-to-date assessment and investigation into the matter, Human Rights Commission on South Africa, "Checkmate for apartheid: Special Report on two years of destabilisation — July 1990-June 1992."

[23] Beaufre, *Introduction to strategy*, 13

[24] Ibid., 23

> Action is total and... must prepare... and exploit the results
> expected from military operations by suitable operations in
> the psychological, political, economic and diplomatic fields.
> Total strategy... consists of the planning and conduct of this
> whole range of actions.[25]

The state, therefore, must bring into play all the resources which it
has at its disposal and involving a mixture of subtle and brutal
technical ingredients ranging from moral coalition to blunt counter-
terror.[26] In practice, anything is possible, any means justified. An
action involving the blowing up of a white spokesperson for the
ANC, who happens to be a priest, is by no means beyond the pale.

Beaufre argues that in practice, this kind of strategy represents "a
tough form of negotiation," which has the aim not so much of
forcing the absolute capitulation of "the enemy" as to "suggest to
him that he should consider as a possible compromise a solution
which accords with our political objectives."[27] If total strategy is to
succeed, there has to be a "continuous osmosis between policy and
strategy" which involves a much greater interchangeability between
the roles of soldier and politician.[28]

Soon after assuming office, De Klerk dismissed the National
Security Management System with a wave of his reformist hand.
Suddenly we had entered the prospect of a New Jerusalem — or at
least a "New South Africa." Anyone who quibbled seemed to be
terribly churlish. The whole country was swept away on a tide of
"reconciliation" and "New South Africa-ism." The genius of the man
was to *appear* to be doing the right thing at every turn; and indeed,
some things he certainly did do right, but in the process he was also
implementing the basic doctrine of counterinsurgency — *both* reform
and repression. You can't have the one without the other, both have
to be real and controlled and must work in the ultimate interest of
the state.

We now have documentary evidence in the case of Matthew
Goniwe, Fort Calata, Sparrow Mkonto and Sicela Mhlauli, (four
popular Eastern Cape activists) that there was an established proced-

---

[25] A. Beaufre, *Strategy of action*, London, Faber and Faber, 1967, 104.

[26] See P. Frankel, *Pretoria's Praetorians: Civil-military relations in South Africa*,
Cambridge University Press, 1984, 49.

[27] Beaufre, *Strategy of action*, 115.

[28] Ibid., 131

ure for authorising political assassinations which involved the very highest councils of government.[29] Furthermore, several of the people who took such decisions relating to cases such as this are still in the Cabinet of the Government of National Unity. Alastair Sparks, former editor of the *Rand Daily Mail* and not known for his radical opinions, muses on the glib government answer, that assassinations and "hit squad" activity on the part of the police are examples of "a few rotten apples":

> It would appear, therefore, that the assassinations carried out in 1985 were not done by "rotten apples" [in the police force] but by trained hit squads acting on orders from above, in accordance with approved policy. This must now be placed in context with the large accumulation of evidence indicating that such hit squad activity is continuing... There is... "a golden thread" running through all the incidents — from the smashing of Alan Paton's car windscreen and the sending of a toxic T-shirt to Donald Woods' small daughter, to the more systematic and ideological operations of the eighties, when the Civil Cooperation Bureau (CCB) hung a baboon foetus outside Bishop Tutu's home, poisoned the Reverend Frank Chikane's clothing, switched lawyer Dullar Omar's heart pills to give him a coronary attack, and went in for selective assassinations.
>
> There was the blowing up of Albie Sachs, the assassination of Ruth First, Jeanette Schoon and her daughter, Griffiths and Victoria Mxenge, Goniwe and his colleagues, Fabian and Florence Ribeiro, David Webster and many more. There was support for Renamo to destabilize Mozambique as an ANC base, the bombs in Zimbabwe, death-squad raids into Swaziland, a clandestine campaign to destabilise SWAPO in the Namibian elections, Inkathagate, the Trust Feeds massacre and its evidence of support for Inkatha in destabilising the legalised ANC inside South Africa... It's a long, long thread of official venality and violence. Yet the evidence disappears into some cosmic black hole in Pretoria and there is no response other than bland assurances that the police are committed to peace and the horrors are the work of a few rotten apples.[30]

---

[29] See "Death order from General," *New Nation*, May 8-14 1992.
[30] A. Sparks, "A legacy of dirty tricks," *The Natal Witness*, May 14, 1992.

We can no longer, in all honesty, swallow the previous government's line, that the massacres on commuter trains and taxis and buses were caused because of the inherent violence of black people — so-called "black on black violence." It is now quite clear that the state developed a systematic plan of consolidating its power by subverting the oppressed and attempting to co-opt their organizations into some form of alliance with itself. This was done in such a way as to make opposition seem hysterical at best, or even heretical. The battle was for the middle ground, and to a very large degree the former government successfully managed to grab it for itself. The fact that the National Party, the party which implemented and maintained apartheid, managed to persuade colored voters in the Western Cape, for example, to vote against the ANC has this "battle for the middle ground" as part of the answer.

The crucial relation between religion and Low Intensity Conflict has been extensively explored elsewhere.[31] For our purposes, it is important to understand that it was essential to national security ideological construction for people to believe, to some extent at the very least in what Jose Comblin terms the myth of the "eternal antagonism between nations."[32] The ideology was founded upon a very simplistic view of the world and history in general — there is good and there is bad, which must be fought. Communists are bad because they are atheists and they want to take what belongs to us in order to further their lust for control and resources. Thus the complexity of the struggle is reduced to a simple decision between good and evil, which is then projected into the international

---

[31] See P. Gifford, *The religious right in Southern Africa*, Harare, Baobab and University of Zimbabwe Publications, 1988; M. Worsnip, "Low intensity conflict and the South African Church," in *Journal of Theology for Southern Africa*, No.69, December 1989, (a more detailed version of this paper was printed under the same title with an introduction by Mark Phillips, *IDASA Occasional Papers*, No.23). This research was used for the production of the international document, *The road to Damascus: Kairos and conversion*, published variously, 1989; U. Duchrow, G. Eisenburger and J. Hippler, *Total war against the poor*, New York, Circus publications, 1990; J. Nelson-Pallmeyer, *War against the poor: Low-intensity conflict and the Christian Faith*, Maryknoll, New York, Orbis, 1990; See also CIIR, *Now everyone is afraid: The changing face of policing in South Africa*, London, CIIR, 1988.

[32] J. Comblin, *The Church and the national security state*, Maryknoll, NY, Orbis, 1979, 170.

geopolitical arena of what used to be East-West relations. In this scenario, the United States and other Western capitalist nations are united against the principal enemy, which was the former Soviet Union and its allies, and today is Cuba, China, and any form of socialism. Biblically understood, what we have is the ancient paradigm of the "heathen" nations ranged against Israel, godlessness ranged against the chosen people. As a matter of "fact," this antagonism is never resolved; the struggle continues until the Parousia, when the whole issue is finally resolved by God.

In this scheme of things the mantel of Christianity was naturally claimed by the state. Indeed in large measure, Christianity was utilized and co-opted by the state for the purpose of legitimizing the state; there was a very real sense in which the State President, in South Africa, became the High Priest of this particular type of selective religion. The dualisms operated fairly comfortably together: the first dictated that there is the realm of the Church and there is the realm of the world, and the two are completely separable. The second operates on a somewhat more ideological level: there is a world of darkness and a world of light. The world of darkness is the "Evil Empire" of the communists and the world of light is the "free" world of the capitalists. These worlds cannot and must not be confused; people and actions can be labelled according to which sphere the state wishes them to belong. In this scheme of things, Liberation Theology or Contextual Theology, for example, is systematically demonised, not so much by the state, but especially by the dominant Church, "mainstream" as well as other.

Here we have to face a very painful fact, so painful, that it is almost too difficult for us to examine at all. It is this: the so-called "rightwing" churches are not a great deal different from the so-called "mainstream" churches, in the end. The theology of the former may well be more crass and unpalatable, but ultimately, there is not a great deal of a difference between them.[33] At one time, certainly while doing the research related to the production of *The road to Damascus*, those of us who were involved reached the conclusion that it was the so-called "rightwing" churches which were the problem. It is horrifying to discover the "rightwing" in our midst!

---

[33] See, for a well argued paper on this issue, C. Villa-Vicencio, "Right wing religion: Have the chickens come home to roost?," in *Journal of Theology for Southern Africa,*No 69, December, 1989.

It was against the background of LIC that Michael developed his argument that the Church, in attempting to be neutral, was in reality co-opted for the designs of the state, especially when this was the strategic and planned intention of the state. However, Michael went further than this and directly blamed the Church itself:[34]

> The shameful history of apartheid is that before it was a political and economic system, it was in the Church. Separation began theologically in the Church. [Theology says to the black person]... "Don't worry that you are oppressed now, heaven is waiting for you." It also tells that black person that the most important thing is a personal relationship with Jesus and to forget about the community and social problems...
>
> The God of the Bible is never neutral. Jesus doesn't say, "I have come to sit on the fence." But rather, "I have come to bring the good news to the poor." The alternative to apartheid theology is new life. The alternative to the apartheid state is a national liberation movement for everyone. All people need to be freed.[35]

The gospel is never neutral — a great number of Christians would agree with this statement. Of course, what it means depends a great deal on one's point of theological departure. For Michael, the point of departure is neither reading the Bible, nor expounding scripture, nor prayer, nor worship, nor the study of Christian doctrine. For him, none of these things constitutes "doing theology" or even "theological reflection," although all of these elements may well have a place in the process. Michael identifies in the bible a "dialectical relationship" with a God who is at once universal and at the same time "partial":

> The Creator is the one who sides with a small group of slaves and makes them an instrument of... liberation. God's involve-

---

[34] Much the same point is made in J. Cochrane, *Servants of power: The role of English-speaking Churches in South Africa: 1903-1930*, Johannesburg, Ravan Press, 1987; and C. Villa-Vicencio, *Trapped in apartheid: A socio-theological history of the English-speaking churches*, New York, Maryknoll, Orbis and Cape Town, David Philip, 1988.

[35] Michael Lapsley, "Gospel a weapon in South Africa," PM, April 16, 1990.

ment in an act of subversion, an act of political rebellion is a central theme of the Old Testament.[36]

In one sense, Michael is theologically typical of liberation theologians the world over; the point of departure is the Exodus event, an event of historical, political, social, cultural and even economic liberation, to be read (and for the hermeneutic to work, it needs to be read) fairly historically in order for it to make any interpretative sense. It ceases to have the impact it should if the story is reduced to the level of legend or fancy, or if it becomes textually and interpretatively out of the reach of the "ordinary reader."[37] It must be read as a literal historical act of divine intervention in order for it to acquire the desired impact; the obvious inference being, if God entered human affairs in that sort of a way, in this instance, then the text is telling us something about the sort of God with whom we are dealing. In any analysis, this is a very traditional, even literal reading of the text. Why does Michael allow such a starting point, given the fact that he is schooled in textual criticism and all the rest?

Michael shares with the *Kairos Document*, a concern to break the stranglehold which the "dominating classes" have on theology:

> Part of the emasculation of the Christian gospel by the theologies of the ruling class involved increasing emphasis on orthodoxy (correct teaching) rather than orthopraxis (correct action rising from reflection).
>
> It is the Latin Americans more than anyone who have liberated theology from the clutches of the dominating classes. Most of Latin America was colonized centuries ago. To a frightening extent Catholic Christianity identified itself with the colonial structures of oppression and exploitation...

[36] Michael Lapsley, "What does it mean to reflect theologically?," Zimbabwe, November, 1986.

[37] I am, to a large extent reliant for language here on the extremely valuable work done by Gerald West on the the topic of biblical hermeneutics of liberation. To my knowledge, West is one of the very few people in South Africa to take seriously the issue of the hermeneutics of liberation. See G.O. West, *Biblical hermeneutics of liberation: Modes of reading the Bible in the South African context*, Pietermaritzburg, Cluster Publications, Monograph Series number 1, 1991. See especially chapter 7.

For the majority of Christians in Latin America, the overwhelming fact of their lives is that they are oppressed. Oppressed people, struggling to remove the shackles of oppression began to read the Bible in a new way. They began to see that God was not neutral but partial, that he is concerned with the totality of human life. They began to rediscover that the test of faith is action.

Christians began to discover the needs for tools of analysis drawn from sociology, psychology and political economy if they were to understand not only the mechanism of oppression, but also the economic and political options of a new society which would embody the values of God's Kingdom.[38]

There is no doubt in Michael's mind that the use of these tools of analysis was one of the great liberating "discoveries" of the theologians of liberation. But "Christians need to do more than analyze... They need to act." It is clear that there will be no action if Christians lamely and fatalistically accept their lot as something preordained by God. Events in history are not foreordained, they are created and made; they are accepted or they are rebelled against. They are not fixed.

The issue of power became, for Michael, a crucial one. It was crucial to understand power dynamics, if one was to alter injustice. One can immediately see how his thinking in relation to the question of power is shaped by his own personal experiences, both in the Church and in society at large. In an article entitled "Towards a theology of people's power," Michael examines some of the issues, particularly as they pertain to the Church:

When there is more than one person there is a question of power. Our attitudes toward power are influenced greatly by how much of it we have. To what degree am I an object about whom other people make decisions? To what degree am I a subject with a power of self-determination or at least a say in the things that most affect my life? We know that even those

---

[38] Lapsley, "What does it mean to reflect theologically?"

who have enough to eat are willing, ultimately, to die for the values of human freedom and dignity.[39]

Michael, in the same article, then considers Jesus' perception of power and ponders the text in Mark 10:45 where the ideal of the Christian is to be the servant, not the one in control. The article then contrasts this perception with the fourth century historical development which saw Christian bishops behaving much more like feudal lords than servants:

> A process was begun which reflected in values, art, architecture and church government, of transposing Christian values with imperial values. To a frightening degree that which the empire valued, which was often in total contradiction to the values of the gospel, began to be called Christian too. Who converted whom, we may ask?[40]

Michael then suggests that the Church today has "various mechanisms" which are used to "disenfranchise the people and prevent the emergence of a people's church." Theology becomes the preserve of academic experts, church leaders and priests, all of whom "have their own interests to preserve." Theological language itself "frequently mystifies rather than elucidates the mystery of God to the ordinary worshipper."

In Michael's own estimation, it was precisely this aspect of his theology, the deliberate decision to make theology "of the people" and to allow people to make their own decisions, which was to prove too difficult for the hierarchy of the Church. What he had wanted to do was to practise in the Church what he fought for in society. In the parish in Harare, Michael attempted to begin from the premise of a "liberatory model of the Church and of the gospel" and see if it could work in a parish situation." He found that it worked "beyond my wildest expectations."[41] When Michael went to St Michael's parish, there were very few youth and mainly middle-aged and elderly women. Within six months, the congregation had quadrupled in size, the youth came back in large numbers, the men

---

[39] Michael Lapsley, "Towards a theology of people's power," *Moto*, No 52, 1987, 20-21.

[40] Ibid.

[41] Michael Lapsley, interview, Pietermaritzburg, July 5, 1992.

returned, and the middle aged and elderly women stayed on. The parish became more representative of the teeming, overcrowded community which was Mbare. Suddenly, the parish exploded into life; people were taking responsibility for their own lives and able to speak for themselves. Michael is very insistent on the fact that "all the conventional things" were done in the church as well. Mass was said every day; all the sacraments of the Church were celebrated; the sick, the elderly, the distressed were visited and ministered to in a very straight-up-and-down conventional way.

However, in addition, the liturgy began to be examined and made more contemporary; the parish was divided into "areas" and each Sunday one of the different geographical areas would be responsible for the liturgy. So it transpired that up to forty different people, every Sunday, would be participating in the liturgy. The Mother's Union identified illiteracy as their greatest need; a local donor funded the training of a literacy teacher from amongst the women themselves, chosen by the women. A community theater group was started amongst the youth, which performed dramas about the problems which the community was facing; these were sometimes performed, instead of a sermon, in the Mass. There were plans to organize a Marimba band and a second choir from amongst the youth; a garden project was begun. These were very simple mechanisms in which every category of person in the parish could begin to feel that it was their parish. The youth had always been told that they were the church of tomorrow; now they began to hear that they were the church of today, together with the elderly, the middle aged, the very young — all are the church of today.

In the parish there were certain tensions around the issues of Church and State, due to the fact that black Anglicans had been given the impression by the Church that their involvement in the liberation struggle was unacceptable. Michael became directly involved in organizing ecumenical services to which the President was invited to preach. He organized Requiem Masses to give thanks for those who had given their lives to free the country. Within the context of faith there was now, for many, an opportunity to own their participation in the struggle for freedom.

As we are all aware, this is not the "normal" face of the Church, which too often considers itself "above" society — and this is very often interpreted to mean "better" than society. This is an exceedingly dangerous, though admittedly very widespread doctrine — that somehow the Church manages to escape the rough and tumble of ordinary human struggle, and as a divine institution cannot be analyzed. Doubtless there is some theology behind the assertion, but it is a theology of the "Kingdom," with everything implied in the way in which Kingdoms are ruled. When, however, we see the falsity of this, when we find ourselves protesting against dictatorial and unjust rule, we discover that we need to go on to apply all the categories which we apply to secular society, to the Church as well. The Church can in no way be exempt from such analysis. It comes as a shock, even as reprehensible to some, to suggest that the Church should, at the very least, be subject to the same norms of justice and freedom as the rest of the world. However, the objection is utterly false, and in the end futile. The Church, like anywhere else, is a "site of struggle."[42]

A great deal of the kind of theology which does not recognize the Church as a site of struggle was both wittingly and unwittingly used in connection with the debate about whether priests of the CPSA should be allowed to belong to political parties or not. Archbishop Desmond Tutu set up the goal posts in an interview he gave to the BBC in June 1990, some four months after the unbanning of political organizations:

> The Church has always got to be one that is uncomfortable with any socio-political setting because it stands for gospel, for Kingdom values, and nowhere in the world would you say that those values are absolutely embodied... We will keep what Latin American theologians call a critical distance, to enable us to say to [political parties]... "Thus saith the Lord. This is wrong, this is right." We couldn't do it if we were ourselves members of that party.[43]

It is in the light of this kind of ecclesiology that the decision of the Synod of Bishops taken in February 1990[44] must be understood. The

---

[42] See M. Worsnip, "Situating spirituality within the struggle," in M. Worsnip and D. van der Water (eds), *We shall overcome: Spirituality for liberation*, Pietermaritzburg, Cluster Publications, 1991.

[43] D. Tutu, Item 248/June 4, 1990, in *Bishopscourt Update*, June 6, 1990, No.6, 1990, 4.

[44] See CPSA *Dispatch*, September 18, 1990, No.39, 1. See also for a similar view to that of Tutu, F. Chikane, "Should the Church take sides?" in *New Era*, Spring 1991, 7ff.

decision was announced in an almost casual way in the May edition of the Cape Town Diocesan newsletter, *Good Hope*:

> We are thankful that political organizations have been unrestricted. The Synod of Bishops has decided though that no licensed ordained person may be a member of any political organization since they should be able to minister to all persons regardless of their political or ideological affiliation.[45]

Not surprisingly there was a great deal of astonishment in the media and not a little discontent in some corners of the Province. The Anglican Students' Federation took a resolution noting with concern the fact that the decision had been made without consultation, as well as protesting the decision itself. The resolution went on to affirm that ministers were "an integral part of our communities" and resolved that they should be "entitled to express their beliefs in the way they feel is appropriate." ASF resolved that the Synod of Bishops should review their decision and "enter a process of consultation."[46] The Archbishop had been invited to speak at the Conference and he explained the bishops' decision in the following terms:

> Just two weeks ago, I was installing the new Bishop of the Diocese of South-Eastern Transvaal, and the servers who had gathered at the end of the service — you know we were singing the National Anthem — you had some with the clenched fist and some with the open palm — meaning that you had people who belonged to PAC (or claimed that they were PAC) and we had people who belonged to the ANC. And if you as the priest come along and you say that "I'm actually PAC," with all the goodwill in the world, there is no way in which people who belong to a party that is opposite to the one to which you have declared yourself, are going to be able to accept openly, readily, your ministrations.
> Imagine when you have someone who is Inkatha and they want to come to confession to a priest they know is ANC.... Our decision does not mean, when the time comes when you

---

[45] D. Tutu, "Archbishop's letter," *Good Hope*, May 1990, Vol XLI No.5.
[46] Anglican Students' Federation, "Minutes of the 30th Annual General Meeting," Resolution 17, 31.

can vote — that you shouldn't vote according to how you have decided yourselves. ...another thing is that we are engaging, as churches, in the process of seeking to be facilitators in the process of negotiation. In this area we have been trying to bring together two groups. We are not playing marbles! I mean people are dying because of the differences between these two groups.... You have to be seen to have a particular kind of impartiality. Of course there is actually no one else, I don't think, who would be able to bring those two groups together. They are willing to accept the good offices — the mediation of the Church... now I've been General Secretary of the SACC [South African Council of Churches]. And I want to tell you the kind of clobbering I had because they said the SACC was one that favored the ANC. We were looking after political prisoners and their families and when one political prisoner — leader — was released, who belonged to the PAC — whom the [SACC]... had looked after in equal measure to other people — when I went to see this man to celebrate his release — I came away with an earful. And only recently, three weeks ago, we were having conversation with different political groups including AZAPO and PAC, and again they are saying there is no question at all about the bias of the SACC. And we are speaking with people who are maybe not hotheaded... I am saying we are not dealing with situations where people have been accustomed to accommodating differences of points of view. It's not the same thing as being (say) in England, where the political affiliation that you have is in a sense an irrelevance. Although even there people would find it difficult perhaps to, say, be accepting of the ministry of someone they knew, say, supported Mrs Thatcher in a miners community. But here! I mean we couldn't possibly jeopardize the possibility of ministry in the kind of way that would happen if you declared your political preference. I hope that as the Church may be able to demonstrate it in this country — maybe this subcontinent, and in the continent at large, that it is possible for people to cohere in one community — holding quite diverse points of view. We've not taken this decision lightly... now you can obviously belong to whatever organization you like. But the moment you are ordained. Then it is a firm instruction [that you should not].[47]

On the question of consultation the Archbishop had this to say:

We are sorry that (maybe) we didn't give opportunity for people to discuss and understand our rationale. It is that we are aware that it is a matter of life and death... And if you are ordained that it is not possible for you to remain an official representative of the Church and to be a member of a political party... Right, now you can raise your questions. Let me just say — It would really be a matter of clarification because it isn't open to revision [laughter]... No! No! It's serious. This is not a laughing matter. It is not a laughing matter. It's not a laughing matter when we have our priests killed. It isn't a laughing matter when you... go into the house of a person and you find you've got a 15-year-old killed. It isn't a laughing matter. And I want you to understand that we have taken that decision very prayerfully and seriously. What we can try to do is to try to explicate it. But it is not open to revision. It is not something that we took lightly. It is because of where we are.[48]

In the August 1990 edition of *Good Hope*, the Archbishop gave a more detailed explanation of the reasons behind the decision:

The Synod of Bishops in February decided to prohibit licensed ordained persons from being members of any political organization. The prohibition affects only those personnel: if you are a layperson, or ordained but retired and no longer licensed then this prohibition does not affect you.

We could have done better in giving a proper rationale for the Bishop's decision. I apologize that our failure to do so has caused unnecessary distress to many. This decision does not prohibit political involvement with your community. We will continue to declare what we believe to be God's will for our situation and condemn injustice and oppression as vehemently

---

[47] D. Tutu, speech to the Anglican Students' Federation, National Conference, Federal Theological Seminary, Pietermaritzburg, Natal, July 7, 1990.
[48] Ibid.

as we have ever done. The point is that when we have done this, we have been motivated, not by any ideology, political or otherwise, but by our commitment to our Lord and in obedience to the imperatives of the gospel of Jesus Christ. And so we have condemned apartheid because of our understanding of the Christian faith...

The Church must be involved politically. There can be no neutrality where there is injustice and oppression. But it can never be aligned with any one political party. An ordained person must be able to minister to all his/her people of all political persuasions. A PAC supporter would find it difficult to accept the ministrations of an ordained person who belonged to the ANC as one example. Political affiliations especially in the black community are a matter of life and death. How can a minister who supports Inkatha work in an ANC area? A UDF-supporting priest had to leave Natal because his life was in danger. Recently Father Victor Africander, who was thought to support the ANC was assassinated in Pietermaritzburg.[49] The receptionist at the Cathedral there was stabbed by a young man who said that action was a message to Bishop Michael of the "ANC" Church.

How long would an Inkatha-supporting priest survive in Bonteheuwel? The United Congregational Church stopped the Revd Allan Hendrickse from functioning as a minister of that Church when he became leader of the Labour Party. When I became Bishop of Johannesburg I resigned as Patron of the UDF and as member of the National Forum in order to minister and be seen to minister in a non-partisan way to all, whatever their political affiliation. And only a non-partisan Church can act as a mediator in the tense and volatile situation in the black community, where we still do not know how to accommodate different points of view. The Church must teach our people that you can differ in your views and still be friends. That is why we have said ordained persons must not belong to political parties.[50]

---

[49] For a rebuttal of this view, see R. Lundie, *Victor*, Brevitas, Pietermaritzburg, 1995.

[50] D. Tutu, "Archbishop's letter" *Good Hope*, August 1990, Vol XLI, No. 8. See also *CPSA Dispatch*, July 31, 1990, No.36, 2.

The Bishop of Grahamstown, David Russell, was one of the few bishops who dealt with the matter in an *ad clerum*. He revealed that the decision had been unanimous (though it needs to be noted that some of the bishops of the Province did not attend that particular Episcopal Synod), and that the bishops had felt that it would be "unhelpful and unwise" for clergy to join political parties. He went on to give more reasons for the decision:

> We believe that in our present context in which the processes of peace are in such a fragile state, and in which people of different political persuasions have so easily turned to violent conflict to settle differences and to enforce their viewpoint, it is all the more important that clergy recognize their special role in the parish situation as reconcilers and peacemakers. The Bishops are of the view that it would not help the process of encouraging and working for democracy and economic justice if the priests were to join different political parties, and so become a potential focus of division in the community. This is not to say that we are neutral as a Church when it comes to Biblical values of justice and truth. But clergy have a very particular role to play, and they can best further the gospel values by remaining outside party political involvement.
>
> Having said this with regard to the role of the *clergy*, we believe that it is right and proper to encourage the laity to be involved in the party political processes with a view to furthering convictions and policies which are in keeping with the gospel. In this context of course, people will join different political parties, and they should be upheld in their right to do so. The Church remains as committed as ever to the conviction that any form of racism is sinful, and in this sense we would be critical of particular parties and policies.[51]

After a period of recovery, Michael had written to the Bishop of Matabeleland, Theo Naledi, to enquire as to his position with regard to taking up his post as assistant priest at Makokoba in Bulawayo, the parish to which he was going on the night of his bombing. He received a reply a month later informing him that there was now "no vacancy in the Diocese to employ another priest...." There was

---

[51] D. Russell, *Ad clerum*, No 3 of 1990, March 15, 1990. Emphasis his own.

"absolutely no possibility of having an extra priest as there was neither accommodation nor money to pay stipend."[52]

Michael was disappointed and immensely saddened. With this door closed, and the South African door opened, due to the events of February 2, 1990, Michael felt the need to write to Trevor Huddleston to ask his guidance and advice on the issue of the decision which the bishops of the CPSA had taken with regard to priests of the Province belonging to political parties. Huddleston replied saying that he found it extremely difficult to know what advice to give Michael. He said that the moment he saw a report of it, he had felt it to be a "very dangerous decision." Like Michael, he could understand the pastoral motivation, but while he could understand, he could not agree. He suggested that Michael should "tell Archbishop Desmond that you cannot return to South Africa and at the same time resign from the ANC." In Michael's case, he suggested, this would be a "virtual impossibility because of the cost of your commitment to the ANC and therefore the cost of appearing to betray it."[53]

Trevor Huddleston told me that this was extremely difficult for him to write, because it appeared to be going against the wishes firstly, of the Archbishop of the Province, and secondly because that Archbishop is Desmond Tutu. His respect and love for Desmond Tutu is immense. The feeling is mutual. Tutu describes Trevor Huddleston as the first white man he had ever met who respectfully greeted his mother, by lifting his hat to her. It was Desmond, the lowly black child, whom Huddleston had visited weekly while he was sick in hospital. It was to a very large measure Huddleston who had inspired Desmond to join the Anglican Church. Trevor is the name of Desmond and Leah's only son. It was, and always has been, a very close relationship, and in no way has Huddleston wanted to cross Desmond Tutu, let alone wholeheartedly oppose him. It was thus with great sadness and great deliberation that Huddleston found himself, some months later, in the unenviable position of having to go against the will of his admired friend and pupil.

When the ANC was about to hold its first legal conference inside South Africa since its banning, it officially invited Trevor Huddleston to be present on that historic occasion:

---

[52] The Rt Revd T. Naledi, letter to Michael Lapsley, November 26, 1990.

[53] The Rt Revd T. Huddleston, letter, to Michael Lapsley, November 29, 1990.

...we think it is absolutely crucial that those stalwarts of the freedom struggle, such as you are, who have given their wisdom, energy and determination to the cause of liberation should, circumstances permitting, take their honorable and rightful place at the conference. You Archbishop Huddleston together with the late Chief Albert Luthuli and Yusuf Daadoo, were the first recipients of the *Isitwalandwe-Seaparankoe...*[54] You are invited *not* as an "external delegate" or "observer" or "expatriate visitor." You are invited as a *full delegate.*[55]

Huddleston, after accepting the invitation from the ANC, wrote as a matter of courtesy, to Archbishop Desmond Tutu, telling him of his plans. Tutu happened to be passing through London some weeks before Huddleston's intended date of departure and told him when they met that he was "uneasy" about his return. Tutu followed this up with a letter, restating his unease and ending with the hope that Huddleston "might be prevented from coming."[56] It was a terrible decision for Huddleston to have to make — "one of the hardest," he said to me: to choose between the wishes of the Archbishop of the Province whom he loved and respected and the African National Congress to whose cause he had devoted most of his life. Huddleston felt, after a great deal of heart searching, that "I had to make my own decision," and that was to attend the conference.

What could the problem have been here, one asks oneself? The problem was that the bishops of the CPSA had made their decision to bar priests from belonging to political parties. Now, all of a sudden, Trevor Huddleston would come back, demonstrating very visibly that it was quite possible for a priest — nay, even a bishop and a onetime archbishop, to belong to a political organization. This might have proved embarassing. When I asked Huddleston whether, in his judgement, this was Archbishop Tutu's concern, he agreed that in his opinion, it was.

---

[54] The *Isitwalandwe* is the highest honor of the ANC. Huddleston received his at the historic occasion of the signing of the Freedom Charter in Kliptown, June 25, 1952.
[55] The Rt Revd T. Huddleston, *Return to South Africa: The ecstacy and the agony,* London, Fount, 1991, 13.
[56] Ibid., 19.

With this in mind, it is not surprising that Archbishop Desmond should have written to Michael in the following way:

> We give thanks to God that you survived and that your spirits remain unbowed. We pray that you will continue to be an instrument of justice and reconciliation.
>
> We certainly would welcome you back, but remember, we have a Synod of Bishops decree (sic!) that no licensed ordained person may be a card carrying member of any political organization; you understand the rationale of that decision.[57]

Soon after this, Michael returned to South Africa, and held a meeting with the Archbishop. He was virtually offered a job on the Cathedral staff in Cape Town. The offer, however, for one reason and another, fell through.

A year later, the Archbishop wrote again to Michael, telling him that the bishops, the Dean and he himself had discussed Michael's situation again and were "delighted" at the prospect of his coming to Cape Town. The letter was, in fact, an invitation to come and work there, almost certainly in a township parish. The letter then went on to describe Michael as "a quite extraordinary icon." "This is not to embarrass you, but you are a wonderful instance of the transforming power of the love of God in Christ..."[58]

The letter continues: "You know, of course, that you will have to foreswear membership of any political party. Perhaps it will be necessary that you give me that undertaking in writing for everybody's sake. You will have noted Inkatha's objection to my co-chairing the signing of the Peace Accord because of my alleged bias towards (even membership of) the ANC. We do not want your ministry subverted by suspicions of political partisanship."[59]

With all due respect, it must be said that this is a very curious letter. Is it even remotely likely that anyone in their right mind would imagine that Michael has no ANC allegiance, if he were to simply "foreswear membership"? Is not the proof of the nonsensical pudding precisely in the fact that the Archbishop himself, although he has publicly foresworn political allegiance and never been a

---

[57] The Most Revd D. Tutu, letter to Michael Lapsley, December 13, 1990.

[58] The Most Revd D. Tutu, letter to Michael Lapsley, October 3, 1991.

[59] Ibid.

member of the ANC, *is still unsuitable* to Inkatha. The position of neutrality has not worked, clearly.

Well, it looked very much like an impasse. The likelihood of Michael "foreswearing" membership of the ANC was, realistically, zero, and rightly so, as was the likelihood of Trevor Huddleston doing the same. It defies understanding how anyone, let alone the Church, could ask them to do such a thing, particularly in the pursuit of the myth called "neutrality."

Michael dealt with the issue somewhat more sensitively this time, realizing, as he put it, the "pastoral concern which motivated this condition." Nonetheless, he wished to point out the particularity of his situation:

> The state gave me indemnity as a member of the ANC, without which, it was made clear that I would not be allowed to enter the Republic. In relation to your condition, because I was not born in South Africa, my legal right to return and live in South Africa is directly tied to my membership of the ANC in terms of the agreements between the ANC and the Government. Ironically, renunciation would forfeit my right to return. I feel sure that you and the other bishops will be sympathetic to my position. At the same time, I would always seek to act with sensitivity and circumspection in relation to your pastoral concerns.[60]

In the light of this, Michael requested the Archbishop to give him Permission to Officiate in the Cape Town Diocese. Eventually, such permission was granted with conditions, such as that Michael should not stand on explicitly ANC platforms in an explicitly ANC role, nor can he carry an ANC card. However, Michael has not been asked to "foreswear" anything at all and he has found this suitable enough to live with. Clearly, Michael's position was a unique one. Clearly, too, the actual carrying of an ANC card means very little indeed, bar sentimental value. Indeed, at a supper at Bishopscourt, before it was finalized that Michael would be coming to work in the Diocese of Cape Town, Archbishop Desmond had, in a somewhat joking manner said, "But of course, you will have to tear up your membership card." Michael replied, also somewhat jokingly, "But I have no hands to tear it up with." Apart from anything else, Michael

---

[60] Michael Lapsley, letter, to The Most Revd D. Tutu, January 27, 1992.

came away from that meeting with a very warm sense of approval from the Archbishop, a sense of celebration, a sense of openness and a sense of affirmation. "When all is said and done," said Michael after the meeting, "Desmond is a patriotic South African — a person not blind to sacrifice or commitment." And I, for one, felt very glad.

❦CHAPTER 6

Healing and belonging

"The problem is, many people who notice that you haven't got any hands, somehow also think you haven't got any brain!"

It is very difficult to imagine what life must be like without hands, for those of us who have them. Every moment, every instant, every nuance and gesture. Our hands fill these and hold them and caress them and touch and stroke and handle. It is trite to say that we take them for granted, but a great deal of our expressing, our feeling, our being is there in our hands, for all the sighted world to see.

Michael has no hands now. He has hooks — clipper-type hooks, elegant in a curious sort of way, but hooks nonetheless. Hooks, both different, but similar. Hooks, with a stainless steel coldness and a chiseled inner rim of rubber. They are attached to pinkish artificial stumps. Not quite the color of his flesh, but a good attempt. Again, both individual, yet similar. These handmade stumps are attached to his own stumps with short straps which hold the handmade stump in place. To avoid chaffing, Michael winds soft cloth around his stumps before he inserts them into his prostheses. The whole strange gear is held on to his body and ingeniously operated by a shoulder halter. If he extends his arm from the shoulder, outward, the hook opens. The hooks are held closed by the force of a number of very strong elastic bands. His grip, in essence, is the strength of the elastic bands.

It is an extraordinary and ingenious mechanism that took a great many attempts to get right. At one stage, the experts declared themselves satisfied (and very weary), but Michael insisted that the product was not good enough. He could touch his right ear with his left hook and his left ear with his right hook, but neither his right nor his left hook could even remotely approach his mouth. "Obviously I was going to starve to death if they had their way!"

When Michael had hands, he was right dominant. Now he is left dominant due to the fact that his left hook prosthesis was the first to be fitted. His brain just accommodated — except for his signature, for some reason. He still needs to sign his name with his right arm.

Michael deals with his hooks now rather like hands. The first time one sees them, they have the fascination of gold or ruby. Once the brain gradually accommodates, they become ordinary. On first meeting, people are very flustered, not knowing what to do — whether to shake the things or hold their hands behind their backs. Michael has learnt to deal with this situation by making the first move towards people and hugging them. They are always grateful, even if they are not the hugging types.

When he sits relaxed in conversation, he hooks the one into the other. It makes a soft, dull, metallic, rubber sound when he does — certainly not a human noise, but it has grown to be part of him. When he talks, he gestures with his hooks, and after a while no one notices.

Michael was told, when he was first having his prostheses fitted, that he would never be able to put them on himself. "And why not?" he said defiantly. It takes him, perhaps fifteen seconds nowadays. Tiny things have made his life more comfortable, like the material loops on his arm straps which pull the velcro together; or the strange looking, but very simple little implement, which Michael calls his "thing which looks like something you would do an abortion with." It is a short six centimetre rod, about one centimeter thick, with a curious oblong-shaped wire attached to the tip. This was designed for Michael to do up the buttons on his shirt. All his zips have simple key ring wire loops on them and he can simply pull them up or down with his hook. Michael can drive a car which has been specially adapted for his needs and this has immeasurably increased his independence. Always with a keen eye for gadgets, Michael has many now which are essential to his comfort (and a few for his pleasure). A simple base on his camera means he can now hold it with ease and take photographs. Simple attachments which fit over the usual spikey shower tap handles, make showering easy. A digital radio which can be preset; a lap-top computer instead of a diary. Michael makes the gimmickry work for him.

Once he was led to a room in a conference center with a "disabled" sign on the door, by a very pleased conference center director. At last there was someone who could actually make use of this spanking new facility! Michael looked around to see what was different. Yes, the door leading to the toilet and shower area was bigger, but he doesn't use a wheelchair, so that wouldn't make any difference. Then he noticed yet another "convenience" — a hand-held shower — the one thing which would have made showering for him impossible. Thanking the hosts for their consideration, Michael hastily, to their bitter disappointment, chose an ordinary room, which he was far better equipped to handle.

One of the very few things which Michael is incapable of doing is removing his false eye in order to wash it every two weeks or so. It is a necessary task for which he needs to enlist the help of someone else. He has learnt to make his needs known, not rudely, or demandingly, but very straightforwardly and specifically. Certain sorts of mugs and drinking glasses do not suit the hooks and Michael will ask immediately for something different if what is offered does not suit. "Do you think you could look for something more 'friendly'?" he will say. Sometimes, of course, there is over compensation. I remember the first time I had a meal with him since the bombing, I leaned over as nonchalantly as I could and cut his food into "bite size" pieces. After a while, Michael looked down and said, "Why are you doing that to my lunch?" There is actually very little which comes on a plate that Michael cannot handle.

Obviously, when Michael walks in the street, people stare. Well, mostly black people stare; white people would like to stare, but their mothers told them it was rude to do so, so they glance and then find something terribly interesting on the other side of the road. How much more human is the other response — to look, and be amazed, to be shocked, to cluck one's tongue in disbelief, to sympathize, deeply, as part of the human community.

Several times on planes, the stewardesses have been so embarrassed by Michael's condition, that they simply pretended he was not on the flight! When drinks were served, Michael wasn't offered anything at all. Supper came only to those around him. Naturally he complained. However, on another occasion members of the cabin crew came up to him and said, "Look, we haven't got a clue what your needs might be or how to assist you, but please let us know and we'll do whatever we can to make your flight as comfortable as possible." (A much more appropriate response.) In Los Angeles, Michael got off the plane to find a wheelchair waiting for him. "Is this for my handluggage?" he asked.

Michael has lost his hands. He will never have hands again. He can still feel them there, even though they are not there. He only has one eye. He will never again have two. No amount of sympathy is ever going to get him back these lost parts of his body. No amount of money can ever replace these things once they have been lost.

There is undoubtedly an obvious parallel between Michael's position and that of South Africa as a whole. What can be the recompense for such loss and suffering? What is the content of reconciliation? How can there be forgiveness without some form of retribution? Michael often comments on those who come up to him after speeches and say how nice it is to see that he has forgiven the people who sent him the bomb. He seldom responds, but muses to himself that he has never mentioned the word "forgiveness." What he says is that he is not filled with bitterness and hatred or self-pity, but rather has grown in faith and compassion and commitment to the struggle. Michael is frequently misrepresented in this way, particularly on the question of amnesty. Ideas about amnesty are, according to Michael, based largely on a cheap theology of forgiveness. He does not say that the death squads should not be forgiven, but if they are, it will be something for the oppressed, for the nation collectively to decide — after confession, not before. The oppressed, and only the oppressed, can make the decision as to what can be done to bring healing to the nation — certainly not the oppressor.

There are many people who expect priests to be non-human; they festoon their priests with expectations that they would shudder to burden any other human beings with. They construct plastic messiahs and then get upset when they begin to melt. However, with Michael, only the very stupid, or the very insincere amongst us would expect him to *simply* forgive — because forgiveness is never simple. It never can be. Forgiveness is a complex human response to an equally complex set of circumstances. It happens rarely and when it does, there are no words to describe it adequately.

Nevertheless, the bombers can never win and Michael cannot allow the deed to rule his life. For this reason, there is no bitterness in him. He is committed, as he so frequently has said, to a gospel of life, not a gospel of death. Whereas the gospel of apartheid forever throws up things to divide people, the opposite celebrates community and passionately defends that sense of human belonging.

Michael has always spoken of three kinds of "family" to which he belongs: his natural family, the Society of the Sacred Mission and the African National Congress of South Africa. His natural family have had to cope with the extraordinary strain of Michael's political commitment. This has been a strain, despite the fact that almost all of his family have supported him personally, completely. The love and the care which his sisters poured out on him when he was hospitalized went way beyond simple family belonging.

Undoubtedly Michael would count amongst his family all those who were part of both his political and religious family, as well as friends who were perhaps neither very much — but friends first and foremost. For many Michael has been a point of contact with the hurly-burly world of international politics, even if they themselves would not particularly want to be involved. For many, too, Michael has been a human point of contact with the South African struggle — people who, although they would wholeheartedly support the cause of freedom and justice, would nonetheless not have a great deal to do with South Africa were it not for Michael.

For the ANC, Michael provided a valuable link with the institutional Church. All too often, particularly during the years of banning and underground work, the ANC was far too easily intimidated by the Church. Few within the ANC hierarchy clearly understood the way in which the Church functioned and very often decisions tended to be made, not on the basis of sound theological or structural analysis, but on the basis of assumption. Here, Michael was a valuable ally to correct errors of judgement and diplomacy and also to provide a focus for those within both the Church and the ANC who needed leadership which encompassed and understood both. During the struggle, the relationship between the ANC membership and Church was essential, but has never been easy.

One must say that SSM, the Religious community to which Michael belongs, has been family indeed to Michael during his period of recuperation and healing. Those within it who disapproved of Michael have either been silent or have changed their views to some extent. It is a terribly sad thing, when such a change of heart occurs because of a bomb or because of the external decisions of politicians such as De Klerk. Now, all of a sudden, membership of the ANC is somewhat passé; it is no longer as demonic, outlandish, unthinkable as it used to be. Now Nelson Mandela's autobiography is read with relish and given happily as a Christmas present. How sad for those members who had to have this trivial insight thrust upon them through force of circumstance, rather than through rational thinking or conviction. It is tragic, because they now just look faintly ridiculous. How sad for them. How sad for the Church, which in no way served to challenge their absurdity.

In July 1991, Michael was honored in a rather unexpected way, with the Queen's Service Medal in New Zealand for service to the community in the countries of Southern Africa. Undoubtedly, he felt a mixture of personal pleasure and political uncertainty, as he commented:

> I did not know what to think or how to respond... Those who received honors tended to be captains of industry and retired army colonels. Certainly not priests who join national liberation movements and defend the moral legitimacy of armed struggle! [1]

He interpreted the honor in a strictly *communitarian* way. The then Governor General, Archbishop Paul Reeves, explained that it was one way in which the people of New Zealand could identify with the struggles and sacrifices of the people of South Africa, Zimbabwe and the rest of Southern Africa. The citation spoke of Michael's "missionary work" about which Michael responded:

> It is true that I have sought to serve the community in South Africa, in Lesotho, in Zimbabwe. It is important for me to say that in large measure, I am a product of what the community has given me, immeasurable riches in human relationships... It is true that I am a missionary. Not, I think, here in Zimbabwe. But whenever I go to New Zealand and within the international community, I travel as a missionary. I travel the world seeking to win and convert the unconverted to the cause of freedom and life for all the peoples of Southern Africa. My message is simple. Apartheid and its policy of destabilisation, is a practice and a heretical theology of death, carried out in the name of the gospel of Life. Therefore it is an issue of faith to be part of the struggle for life and peace. Perhaps that is why Pretoria's death squads sought to take my life, but ironically, underlined the truth of what I say. [2]

Michael's life and present disfigurement throws into sharp relief for everyone, the things they would rather avoid. It would be easier if

---

[1] Michael Lapsley, "Speech by Father Michael Lapsley SSM at his investiture with the Queen's Service Medal," Harare, July 13, 1991.

[2] Ibid.

we who are fully limbed never had to deal with others without. Life would be considerably more agreeable if poverty did not exist, or starvation never threatened or squatters never squatted. The architects of grand apartheid tried so desperately to create for themselves a world without ugliness. The people whom one could not cope with, or relate to, or feed or clothe or educate, were carefully relegated to a place out of sight, in the "bantustans" or the kaffirstadt. Despite their efforts, the sky grew darker and the sea rose higher, no matter how much ears were stopped and eyes turned away; no matter how much revulsion and bigotry and fear held sway. The movement towards the truth was inexorable and relentless, and there must come a time when the nightmare fades completely and when peace becomes a strident reality.

Michael's injuries point to the world of those who dominate and say: Behold and beware! As he waved his stumps at the South African trade missions and embassies in the capitals of the world, he reminded us all that apartheid was far from dead, even though Nelson Mandela was out of jail, even though the ANC was about to govern. He bears on his body the continued marks of suffering. He is a symbol, whether he likes it or not, and whether others like it or not, of the suffering people of South Africa — nay — the continent of Africa, Africa wounded, Africa maimed. Africa with nothing to draw the eyes of the smug, intact and comfortable "West" to a more pleasant vista.

Many South African whites want Michael out of the way, and many in the Church would like him out of the Church. Michael makes them see the things about themselves which they would rather avoid, what they don't want to see, and they hate him for doing so. His injuries silence them, but their feelings remain the same.

There is a passage in Dostoyevsky's masterpiece, *The brothers Karamazov*, which has haunted me for many years. When thinking about Michael, my mind keeps returning to the part when two characters, Ivan and Alyosha, are locked in theological debate. Ivan is the sceptic, Alyosha the believer. Ivan relates an incident about a mother forced to witness her son being torn to pieces by dogs because he had injured the paw of the landowners favorite hound. The landowner ordered the entire estate out to watch the spectacle "to teach them a lesson." The landowner/general is later deprived of the right to administer his estates as a punishment for what he had done. "Well," asks Ivan, "what was one to do with him? Shoot him?

Shoot him for the satisfaction of our moral feelings?"[3] The passage ends with Ivan saying:

> But how, how are you to expiate them? Is it possible? Not, surely, by their being avenged? But what do I want them avenged for? What do I want a hell for torturers for? What good can hell do if they have already been tortured to death? And what sort of harmony is it if there is a hell? I want to forgive. I want to embrace. I don't want any more suffering. And if the sufferings of children go to make up the sum of sufferings which is necessary for the purchase of the truth, then I say beforehand that the entire truth is not worth such a price. And finally, I do not want the mother to embrace the torturer who had her child torn to pieces by his dogs! She has no right to forgive him! If she likes she can forgive him for herself, she can forgive the torturer for the immeasurable suffering he has inflicted upon her as a mother; but she has no right to forgive him for the sufferings of her tortured child. She has no right to forgive the torturer for that, even if her child were to forgive him! And if that is so, if they have no right to forgive him, what becomes of the harmony? Is there in the whole world a being who could or would have the right to forgive? I don't want harmony. I don't want it, out of the love I bear for mankind. I want to remain with my suffering unavenged. I'd rather remain with my suffering unavenged and my indignation unappeased, even if I were wrong.[4]

I fear, very greatly, that years of bad, or really inconsequential theology, have led the Church in South Africa (I dare not speak of elsewhere) down the path of cheap thinking. Because vital theological issues have not been faced as they should have been — fairly and squarely — the Church has been able to present to the world a visage of unimpeachable and heroic statements (and indeed some actions) against apartheid, while the rest has been ignored. A great deal of the content of the Church's theology in this neck of the woods has been sadly, tragically, second or even third rate. The result has been, in many instances, a theology shorn of its more

---

[3] F. Dostoyevsky, *The brothers Karamazov*, (Tr. D. Magarshack), Vol.1, Harmondsworth, Penguin, 1958, 284.
[4] Ibid., 287.

ambiguous qualities: a theology chockfull of answers; a theology to appease and please, to warm and uplift; a theology full of certainty and assuredness; a theology which assures the believer of a place in heaven and peace at the last. All these things it has done, but it has never given people the honesty to doubt and to loathe. It has called for forgiveness where none is even remotely possible. It has appealed for reconciliation, where what is required is something far more brutal and perhaps even more sanguine.

Jesus on his cross. Here is a picture indeed, to contemplate: there is the blood, the sweat, the tears; there is the agony of the innocent; there is the familiar group of co-sufferers; there is the mother of the child whose essential humanity is being violated before her eyes; there is the naked Messiah hanging exposed and bleeding on the tree. "Father forgive..." The question which needs asking is: does Jesus himself forgive his persecutors? Does he really? That is what we are told happened, but reading the accounts again and again, one finds nothing of the sort. The forgiveness for which he pleads, does not come from him. Perhaps it may come from somewhere else, but not from him.

Can we forgive? Do we have the right to forgive? What does it mean to forgive? I have no answers to these questions. I am part of the dilemma, after all. I have two hands and I have two eyes. Even though apartheid may well have damaged my humanity and my mind, it has, at least, left my body intact.

There is a well-worn, but nonetheless profound, African phrase which gets trotted out in circumstances of cultural antagonism: "A person is a person through other people." In a word — *ubuntu*. Indeed, I have noticed a certain triumphalism when the phrase or the word is produced. It is used to capture the essence of African communalism. The sense of human belonging and togetherness, of responsibility for the wellbeing of others. The epitome of all that is opposed to "Western" white European individualism — doubtless, a wonderful ideal. Who would want to quarrel with it? Certainly no one in the Church. The tragedy is that the ideal is generally no longer honored, other than with the lips. It is an easy way for Africans who are prey to as much individualism as any "Western" European white, to pretend that they are not. Though I cannot pretend to understand the depths of the concept, I can recognize when it is being practiced and when it is not. The Church, certainly the so called "mainstream" Church, is wrapped up in a "Western" theological framework, the sort of theology which comes from the universities of Europe, often in the original German. Far too many of the people at the top are African only when it suits them. The rest of the time they are as "Western" as Coca-Cola, though they would rather take poison than admit it.

Michael is not an African. He is not an African, despite the fact that from the very core of his being, he might wish he were. He is not, despite the fact that he has chosen to identify with the African cause to the point of near destruction. However, though he might not be an African, Michael belongs to Africa. Michael is one of Africa's wounded children. He is, in many respects, typical of the many (or maybe there are not so many) whites who find themselves incapable of any other real belonging. Once Africa has entered the bloodstream and become part of the fiber of one's being, the path is set and it is frequently a path of suffering.

Truth to say, "belonging" means more than sitting through endless funerals of distant relations. Belonging means sacrifice, and it is this which the Church has neglected to demand of its members. It is one thing to pray for peace, yes even to fast for peace. It is quite another, to sacrifice for peace.

❦CHAPTER 7

"We are the treasure"

To say that Michael's readjustment to the South African Church was an easy one would be understating the truth. Consider the fact that he was very well-known in exile, although inside the country he was less known. A lot of distance gets put between the past and the present very quickly. Occasionally, white clerics knew of him by report, as did some black ones. Where he was known in the Church, he was almost universally regarded as a radical. Now there was the inevitable element of pity because of his hooks. It all added up to the standard recipe for patronizing and avoidance.

There was another element also: Michael had actually lived in South Africa for a relatively short time. It is one thing to live in Lesotho, or Zimbabwe or Zambia, and quite another to come to terms with a country which one has really known from the outside, and a Church as well.

The Church in South Africa, after having been dragged kicking and screaming into the dust and smoke of the struggle, was now only too happy to return to its traditional sanctuary. This was by no means a tremendous shift, because the majority in the Church had never been involved in the struggle in any case.

At the same time, politically acute and active people were for some time now seen to be leaving the Church in their droves. The protection which it had afforded was no longer necessary and they went, black and white, men and women into more relevant sites — universities, schools, the state departments, development — wherever. The seminaries, particularly the mostly black ones, which had been the breeding grounds for political activists in the 1960's and 1970's, were now left, by and large, with an odd and rather unexciting assortment of staff and students, either extremely religious or extremely ambitious, or on occasion, both. In general, they seemed to lack the insight, the sheer capacity of those who had come and gone before and sheltered under the apron of Mother Church, and hence they became sad places with a glittering past and a rather bleak future.

During the struggle years there had been a fairly small cabal within (and to some extent without) the institutional Church. It was a group of people which kept in fairly regular contact with the ANC through many and various underground methods. This group was perhaps most famous for producing, as if from a hat and under the nose of the security police, such worldwide famous documents as *The Kairos Document*[1] and the less well-known *The road to Damascus*.[2] *The Kairos Document* was a deeply revolutionary document in that it presented a radical critique of two forms of theology, namely "State Theology" and "Church Theology," which it claimed were the prevalent theologies of the time. Opposed to these it identified "Prophetic Theology," which it viewed as biblical and in itself a radical critique of the other two. Furthermore, it paved the way for an analysis of the Church as a "site of struggle."

The state correctly saw *The Kairos Document* as a direct full frontal attack and took whatever action it could to stop both the document and the people who had written it. The institutional Church, likewise, understood the message of the document and tried its best to ignore rather than fight it.

There were some complaints from Church activists outside South Africa that they were beginning to feel left out and one can readily understand why. A whole new language and culture of Christian struggle was developing inside the country. The Church came to be identified as "a site of struggle" and it was consequently very directly targeted. Many a bishop knew exactly what was going on and they were not about to encourage it because the finger inevitably pointed directly and unwaveringly at them. What developed was a definite sense of hostility and suspicion on the part of the hierarchy towards that class of priests, ministers and laity who were evidently more interested in "the struggle" than they were in God. They were sidelined or ignored, their faith was often belittled. At no point, however, did the institutional Church manage to create a united front against apartheid. Seldom were people who joined the

---

[1] *The Kairos Document: Challenge to the Church*, The Kairos Theologians, Braamfontein, 1985.

[2] *The road to Damascus: Kairos and Conversion*, Institute for Contextual Theology, Braamfontein, 1989.

liberation movements or the mass democratic movements supported by the Church. Frequently organizations such as the South African Council of Churches and the South African Catholic Bishops Conference were used by churches and prominent individuals to hide behind, while they themselves did very little. In other words, there was a great deal of lip-service to democratic ideals, but very few resources were employed to support and advance them.

Michael came back to the Church in South Africa with a history that stuck to him like glue. In an interview for a position in Kwazulu-Natal, he was asked the question, "Do you still believe in God," almost as though any connection with the ANC would inevitably mean a loss of faith. The problem was, he was also impossible to simply ignore. To employ him in anything like a traditional role, frankly would be very difficult. His political history was, of course, only one part of the problem. Michael recalls a bishop asking him, "But now you are disabled... what can you do?" Michael describes himself as being "still haunted a little bit by that."

> He is a bishop, a leader, a Christian leader, a good man, a good human being. But now I am suddenly a victim. He feels sorry for me, very sorry indeed. I said, I think I can be more of a priest with no hands than I ever was with two hands.[3]

In many of Michael's speeches, he refers to an Eastern Orthodox picture of Christ which shows Jesus as having one leg shorter than the other:

> It's a fascinating image, because if you think of traditional Christian art, Jesus is depicted as the perfect white male body. But here is a picture of Jesus disabled. It picks up an image in Isaiah of a Messiah as one who is not beautiful and comely to look at but rather one who is disfigured. For me, it was an important image to hold on to.[4]

To be sure, I remember looking around the classroom walls of a Catholic Secondary School in Roma, Lesotho. In each classroom was a mandatory picture of Jesus — not always the same picture, but

---

[3] Michael Lapsley, "Speech on disability," Tygerberg Association for the Physically Disabled, April 1994, 7
[4] Ibid., 3.

always a long-haired, blond, white, blue-eyed Jesus, pointing exhibitionist-like to the center of his chest where a red heart-like thing with a sort of a crown on it certainly drew your attention. Jesus always looked a little weak and worn out. It was difficult to know what to make of him, but there was absolute clarity about his color, even though his sex might be a little ambiguous.

On one occasion, I asked the pupils in one of the classes I was teaching to describe to me what Jesus looked like. They didn't need to think about it; they simply pointed to the picture on the wall. That was what Jesus looked like. Jesus was white, they were black. Jesus had long, straight, blond hair, they had short curly black hair. Clearly Jesus was not one of them, and they rejected with contempt any suggestion that Jesus might be represented in any other form.

Later on, when I was teaching in a mostly black seminary, I commissioned a large batik to be hung in the chapel. It was a glorious Ascending Christ, rising from the township slums. The Jesus was uncompromisingly black. The students hated it. They didn't exactly say they wanted a white Christ — that would have plainly been absurd — but many of them had that quaint Victorian picture by William Holman Hunt called "Light of the World" of Jesus standing and knocking at the door of the soul, holding a lantern. It was always prominently displayed in their rooms and that said enough. It was not simply a question of sentimental religion. It was years of a dominant ideology of "to be human is to be white" that also became transformed into "to be God is to be white."

The picture of a perfect, white, male Christ is, doubtless, an alienating one, because in the dominant Western culture within which we all live, Hollywood and not commonality has set the icon of what it means to be human. Many people wanted to know from Michael (and some just wanted to know and wouldn't have been so indiscreet as to ask) how children would relate to him. In his experience, it was not the children who had the problem, rather it was the adults.

The kids always get it right. Children see people. They see me and they say, "It's a bit funny, he hasn't got hands. Where are they hiding? What happened to them?" They want to look sometimes and see where they are. But at the same time, they have no doubt that I am a person. It's the parents who tell them to be quiet and not to ask.[5]

Michael rapidly came to the conclusion that "disability is actually the norm of the human community, not the exception":

I would ask any of you, is there anyone who would be willing to say that there is no part of my life that needs some kind of healing. I wonder if anyone is brave enough to say, "I am a totally whole human being. I have got it all together." That is not the human story. For some of us it is more dramatic and visible. For others it is internal and sometimes much more difficult to address.[6]

To illustrate the issue of power and the way in which those who consider themselves "whole" can often abuse those whom they consider "disabled," Michael recalls an instance where as part of his "rehabilitation" a particular woman asked him to tie together a piece of string. He was not told why he should do this, but in any case he did it — perfectly. He was then told to do it again. He said, "No," he would not do it again. The woman then told him that if he did not do it again, he would be "in trouble." He responded, "I look forward to that."

I was able to say "No." Other people might not have had the confidence to have said "No" and might have been intimidated into continuing with the nonsense. For me it was a very important little incident in terms of the sorts of relations that can develop in any kind of helping profession. Relationships that do not respect the integrity, the dignity and the right to self-determination of individual human beings.[7]

The real sense of disability occurs when people do not treat you as a person first and foremost. Michael recalls visiting some people with a friend of his. The woman they were visiting started speaking to his companion asking if this or that cup would do for Michael — in his

[5] Ibid., 6.
[6] Ibid., 4.
[7] Ibid., 5.

presence, giving him a real sense of having been robbed of his personhood.

Of course, millions of black South Africans will find this nothing unfamiliar in a country where, until now, to be human was to be white, and where black men and women were universally reduced to the status of "boys" and "girls." Domestic workers were spoken about in the most degrading ways imaginable in their presence by white employers. They were not people, they were "Kaffirs," "Munts," "Coons," "Houts," "Shogs," "Wogs," "Zots," "Flatnoses," "Niggers" and now (wait for it) "Dark greens." The difference between then and now is that now we have a Constitution that guarantees the right not to be discriminated against. This is a tremendous change, although it will take some time to be felt. It will take some time before people start to respect the humanity in those around them, but it is there and it is not going to go away. The difference is, that now people have a Constitutional right to be treated with dignity and humanity, black or white; old or young; woman or man; gay or straight; disabled or not. That is a tremendous change. In the end, it was this for which the long struggle was waged. In the end it was for this that children were shot in Soweto. In the end it was for this that they left the country to be trained in foreign lands to return to the crying, beloved country to be shot, or tortured, or hunted, or killed — or to survive, of course, as millions have done. Millions have survived into the present. Millions, through sheer grit and will, have not allowed themselves to be cowed into submission.

Michael is fond of making the point himself, very strongly, that he does not want to see himself simply as a victim or a survivor:

> I realized that if I became filled with hatred, bitterness, self-pity and desire for revenge, I would remain a victim forever. It would consume me. It would eat me alive. God and people of faith and hope enabled me to make my bombing redemptive — to bring life out of the death, the good out of the evil. I was enabled to grow in faith, in commitment to justice, in compassion.[8]

[8] Michael Lapsley, interview, BBC Radio, April 13, 1995.

He shares this extraordinary position with the millions of South Africans who have had their dignity and rights systematically stripped from them:

> I am no longer a victim, nor even simply a survivor. I am a victor over evil, hatred and death... Within the country, there was psychological and physical torture on a massive scale. The apartheid regime and all who supported it carry responsibility for the loss of millions of lives throughout the whole region of Southern Africa.[9]

Michael once ended a talk he was giving to the Tygerberg Association for the Physically Disabled by retelling the story of St Lawrence who, on being asked by the prefect of Rome to deliver to him the treasure of the Church, gathered together the very poorest and presented them to the prefect. "These," he said, "are the treasure of the Church." For Michael, it is the disabled who are the treasure, not only of the Church, but of the world, because they point towards a reality of human interdependence and hope in themselves. They bear in their bodies, the healing marks of Christ. They bear in their lives rejection and suffering. They are the treasure. To understand this is to live victoriously.

One of the major realities which faced Michael on his return, was the question of indemnity. The way things were, there would be no other way to return except by receiving indemnity from the state. The issuing of indemnity from the De Klerk government posed, not only for Michael, but for all other returnees, serious and ironic dilemmas. Speaking at a meeting convened to oppose the Further Indemnity Bill and a General Amnesty in Cape Town in October 1992, Michael had this to say:

> In February of this year, I came back to live in South Africa. Before I could enter South Africa, I was required to obtain indemnity. I was given indemnity. I am a priest, not a lawyer. I understood that they were forgiving *me* for *their* sins. What was the sin that I and thousands like me had committed? What was our crime? We dared to believe that God had created us all equal, with an equal right to a place in the sun. We dared to believe in our common humanity and we strove to live

---

[9] Ibid.

accordingly. We knew that South Africa belongs to all who live in it, so we began to create a non-racial society in our places of exile. As a result, throughout the states of Southern Africa, the regime hunted us down like wild animals.

With the taxpayers' money from the pockets of all South Africans, war was declared not only on the South African people, but was exported to the whole region. The regime financed, supplied and trained bandits, especially in Angola and Mozambique [wars that have] made Mozambique the poorest country in the world and left Angola with more amputees than any country in the world. All in the name of Christianity. In 1990, the policy of destabilization was brought home to South Africa and used domestically, causing the deaths of thousands. That is why we say that apartheid was and is an ideology of and an option for death.[10]

"And now," Michael continued, "they have decided to forgive themselves." He wondered how it was possible for him to forgive people who had neither asked for his forgiveness, nor admitted their fault. The logic of the Bill was that everyone would be treated fairly — ANC and government alike. That is how it was presented and, on the surface, that is what it looks like. However, Michael asked, "Is it fair that a man who commits rape should be treated [in] exactly the same way as a woman who defends herself against rape?"

As a community, we are right to condemn abuses committed by the ANC in the course of a just struggle against what the world calls a crime against humanity. However, to say that the crimes of the state and its agents are no worse than what was done by the ANC may be acceptable to some members of the white community, but God, history, the international community and those who have been victims, will not absolve the regime so cheaply and easily.[11]

On one occasion, a visibly shocked white woman came up to Michael and said to him, "Are you telling me that my government sent you a letter bomb?"

---

[10] Michael Lapsley, speech, to the meeting to oppose the Further Indemnity Bill and a General Amnesty, Cape Town, October 19, 1992
[11] Ibid.

To what extent white South Africans do not know the level of atrocity which was conducted in their name and with the aim of their "protection," is a very difficult thing to tell. After all, decade after decade saw white boys 18 years and upwards standing at railway stations, being prised from the arms of proud mothers and weeping girlfriends by (for the moment) benign looking corporals to start their military training. Off they went, and when they came back, muscle-bound with cropped hair, they told stories clutching beer cans, of the "terrs" and "gooks" they had killed and the victories they had won. They all had a cruel and harsh look in their eyes and they hated blacks, even if they had only been lukewarm before. They were certain of their role, their apocalyptic and lonely role, to protect the country — perhaps even the world — from Communism, and South Africa from a black government. Wives, mothers and girlfriends would listen attentively and tend to their every need. Proud fathers, in-awe younger brothers and next-door neighbors would afford them every possible indulgence on their weekend passes. Of course, there were things they were "not allowed to discuss," which they would always let you know they were not allowed to discuss. Boys suddenly acting with the secret *gravitas* of a war general. Occasionally they would break down and cry, remembering a colleague shot dead in front of them, a helicopter blown out of the sky.

It is true that everyone got caught up in the nightmare. However, did ordinary whites actually know the extent to which atrocity was being committed in their name? That, I really don't know. But *someone* must have known.

Michael recalls meeting his psychologist in Australia for the first time. She was white and she was a South African. Michael had no problem about this, but on hearing what had happened to him, the psychologist felt an overwhelming sense of culpability for the deed. Michael's bombing became a personal crisis for her, and he found that he became priest to her predicament, Father confessor to her felt sin. It was an extraordinary reversal of roles that did not continue for very long as she felt incapable of helping him.

So, how much did white South Africans know about what was happening around them? Michael has no doubt that someone knew and that someone is guilty:

> Whilst apologizing for apartheid... in Winburg, De Klerk said,
> "But that we were evil, malignant and mean — to that we say

'No!'" With all due respect, I would like to tell Mr De Klerk today, that until he and his supporters admit and repent of their evil, malignancy and meanness, they will never be free and it will haunt them, even for generations to come. In Christian theology, evil has to be confessed, repented of and restitution has to be made to victims and communities. Revenge is not the Christian way, justice is. Saying sorry for death and suffering and then staying in power is a contradiction in terms.

Am I wrong to hold President De Klerk personally responsible as well as his government, for attempted murder, in my own case? In the face of the revelations about the CCB, the State President continued to express his unqualified confidence in the security forces... after February 2. What actions did President De Klerk take to disband the death squads which were and maybe still are part of the official machinery of the state?...

Before healing can take place, before we can decide what to do with those who have confessed and repented of their crimes against humanity, power must change hands.[12]

It is true that very few of us had any real idea that then President De Klerk would make his famous announcement on February 2, 1990. Few inside or outside the country expected it. Once made, it was very apparent to everyone that radical action needed to be taken almost immediately. Exiles who had thought of themselves dying abroad now had to think of returning to the country. *Umkhonto* soldiers had to think about integration with the South African Defense Force and vice versa. Whites had to reconcile themselves to a democracy. Homeland leaders had to suddenly fend for themselves. They were heady days indeed.

White South Africa, in general, appeared perfectly able to adapt. Sure, there were some worries. The impossible — what had never been allowed to happen for the sake of Christianity, culture, civilisation etcetera — was now a looming prospect. Nelson Mandela was walking out of Victor Vester Prison, smiling and waving to the world, with Winnie on his arm. It was astonishing, but it was happening. As time passed, it became more and more difficult to find whites who had supported apartheid in any way. With considerable

---

[12] Ibid., 3.

beneficence and easy largesse, South African whites became citizens of "the New South Africa," but it was often extremely difficult to see how "the New" differed from "the Old." In February 1992, Michael had this to say:

> I was struck by the glibness of the dominant media and many whites when they talk of "the New South Africa," as though it was just like putting on a clean shirt without any understanding of the scale of past and present suffering. They speak of wanting a democratic state, but on their terms and in a way that allows them to keep their power, privilege and wealth. They do not seem to recognize the deep need for the transformation of the structures of society as well as individual hearts and minds.[13]

After his return to South Africa, the immediate imperative for Michael was to find some suitable place to work. He approached several bishops of the CPSA with varying degrees of success. Archbishop Desmond Tutu was, as I have already said, more than pleased to have Michael working in his Diocese. As it happens, Michael decided to take a post as Director of the Theology Exchange Program (which became the Center for South-South Dialogue) in Cape Town. At the same time, very soon after his return, he was again elected National Chaplain to the Anglican Students' Federation (ASF). It was poignant to have a whole new generation of (mainly black) students recognizing once again the extraordinary qualities which Michael had to share. Michael accepted the position and threw himself into it with his usual vigor. Consequently, the ASF was strengthened and grew, and during Michael's tenure as National Chaplain started to gain an unprecedented credibility and stature in the Province.

Certain things needed to come together to allow this to happen, and as it turned out they did — such as the new acceptability of the ANC in the country. Nevertheless, the heirarchy was still somewhat shy of direct political involvement and extremely wary of Michael's influence. However, to everyone's surprise, Michael concentrated on quietly building the organization and spirituality. National conferences were profoundly spiritual affairs with an uncompromising

---

[13] Michael Lapsley, "Hope for South Africa but apartheid remains," in *Partners*, The Australian Board of Missions publication, Vol.8-No.1, February 1992.

accent on Bible study and Eucharist. Of course, they also dealt with a range of other issues, such as the environment, AIDS and human sexuality, politics and suchlike, but the spiritual context was extremely clear. The position also enabled Michael to get to know the South African Church again, from the inside, and to interact with a very wide range of students and clergy from across the Province.

Michael came into contact with many people through ASF and his other work. For one young man, this contact was to be life-changing. He wrote a letter, which was subsequently broadcast on the BBC. It is an extraordinary letter that speaks of the pain and the glory of living in these times:

Dear Ninja,

You'll probably be surprised to receive a letter from me. I've never written to you, in fact we've never had a decent conversation.

But I need to talk to you about an incident which, for a chilling moment, brought our lives abruptly together. I doubt whether you'll still remember it. But for me, it proved to be a turning point in my life.

It was the third year of the State of Emergency. More and more people were beginning to say "no" to the brutality of the then apartheid regime. People from all walks of life, from all communities, were actively opposing apartheid and refused to be part of such a demonic system. The government was getting desperate and needed a new mandate however un-democratic and subversive their tactics were going to be. So, on September 6, 1989, they called for a municipal election.

All over the country, the regime started to put their armed machinery in place; in almost every township troops or police were out in force. And all over the country, the demon-strations began.

The fateful morning, students of Macassar also took to the streets. Clashes were inevitable, and I saw how the police, of which you were one, treated those who were exercising their God-given right to protest. The most horrific thing I witnessed that day was you chasing with a sjambok one high school pupil. I was totally appalled at the absolute callous beating you were inflicting on a sixteen-year-old boy. I somehow knew that I or anybody else for that matter had to do something to stop the unnecessary beating of that child. So, I began to shout, begging you to stop. I was relieved to see that my shouting had some kind of effect on you, as you did stop hitting the child. My relief was short-lived, however, as you retreated in my direction. You took out your gun and pointed it at me. At that point all I could think of was the words of the ANC slogan: "Freedom or death — victory is certain."

I believe that you did intend killing me that day. My suspicion was confirmed the following day, when I learnt that on that day about six people died at the hands of the South African police. I hated you. Not only because you wanted to kill me, but more for what you represented. We were both from the same community. We were both regarded as coloreds. And yet you chose to align yourself with an institution that was morally bankrupt, made up of people who took pleasure in the death of their fellow South Africans. God knows, but if it wasn't for those people who were around us, calling for sanity on your behalf, I would have died. You would have killed me.

Last year, we had our first democratic elections. For the first time we as South Africans did something together. As I made my cross, I thanked God that we as a nation had a second chance. I think we also had a unique opportunity to commit ourselves to build a nation.

After that incident, I hated you. Not only because of the fact that you wanted to kill me, but also because you never attempted to ask for my forgiveness or render an apology. Although I was obviously quite pleased about the fact that about six months after than incident, the Movements were unbanned and Mandela and others being freed, still I carried this grudge inside of me. It was not until I saw a video of an Anglican Priest who was bombed and survived the attack, that I wanted to relieve myself of this burden that was eating inside me. This priest astonished the world with the prophetic message of reconciliation. For the first time I saw that I was consumed with anger, hatred and bitterness. All I want to do is forgive you, not only in an attempt to rid myself of this burden, but I believe that this is the only way for true and meaningful reconciliation.

I am not bitter anymore. Yet I believe that in order for true reconciliation to take place, I need to say publicly: I forgive you. We belong to the same community. We both love the people very much. Let us come together, in spite of our difference, to build our community and our nation.

I hope that you will respond favorably to this letter.

Yours sincerely

Johan Magerman
24 March 1995[14]

The election in April 1994 was an almost sacramental event in South African history, despite being preceded by the most extraordinary level of paranoia, rumour and uncertainty. Whites in particular throughout the country started stocking up with supplies to prepare themselves for the expected siege when banks would be closed, electricity and water switched off, shops would be looted and no one would be able to go out of doors.

Normally level-headed people gathered their tinned sardines, paraffin lamps, frozen vegetables (to what end one wondered, if the electricity was going to be switched off!), powdered milk and other necessary items. The supermarkets and shopping malls throughout the country simply could not keep up with the demand and were faced with empty shelves on a daily basis. Of course, the gun shops weren't complaining either.

Then the day arrived, a day of peace and calm, as quietly, good-humoredly and with almost indescribable dignity, the people of South Africa went to the polls to vote in the first democratic election in the history of the country. It became clear from the moment the polling stations opened that there would be no violence; that the tins of sardines and powdered milk had been bought in vain, and that peace and a level of tolerance and goodwill only dreamed of before would rule the day.

There was no sense of bravado anywhere, no gloating or recrimination. There was simply a desire for peace, stability, wholeness, acceptance.

---

[14] J. Magerman, "All I want to do is forgive you," interview, BBC Radio, April 13, 1995.

It was a sacramental moment, and it felt good to be South African. For the first time, the terrible wounds started to feel better — not well, just better.

Michael wrote an open letter to his brethren on his feelings on that day:

> As the day approached, I could not help feeling very emotional, as the full historic significance of the elections dawned on me. Like many people in the country, I felt very excited as the day drew closer. At the same time we are very conscious of the very large number of lives that have been sacrificed to bring us to this moment.
>
> By 6:30 a.m., we had arrived at the polling station, which was only due to open at 7:00 a.m. By 7:00 a.m., the queues were already stretching down the street. The *Cape Times*, which is a morning newspaper, had requested to photograph me voting. They gained special permission to enter the polling station and photograph me as I cast my vote. I decided, because of the great religious significance of the vote for all South Africans, that I should wear my religious habit (appropriately, the caption under the photo was headlined: "Sacred Moment"). The mood of the people was quite lovely with a quiet joyfulness pervading the voters.
>
> Although there were many technical problems during the voting, it is clear that there was an overwhelming response from all over the country. Even the bombs that have gone off have not deterred people in their determination to have a say in how the country should be run and to choose for ourselves the kind of future which we want.
>
> There is a sense in which South Africa will now begin its history as a nation. April 27 is the watershed in a process which will begin to unfold and will take the next couple of generations for all the vestiges of apartheid to disappear. It is extraordinary to realize when we voted, that it was the first time we have ever done something together as one people since 1652.[15]

---

[15] Michael Lapsley, letter to the Brothers of the Society of the Sacred Mission, May 21, 1994.

There was, however, one slight snag: the invisible ink which was applied to each voter's hands in order to detect double voting, proved to be a something of problem in Michael's case. Eventually, the returning officer marked Michael's identity papers to show that he had voted.

For many people the election was a strange and somewhat odd occurrence. The vast majority of people in the country had never voted before. Voting had always been something which whites did alone. It had no significance, no meaning. Nothing ever changed in any case. It was only in Kwazulu-Natal where a note of discord was struck, with gross irregularities and figures which only extreme supporters of Inkatha could believe. Nevertheless, the result for Kwazulu-Natal was accepted, despite the fact that it was highly unsatisfactory to many, perhaps most. However, it was accepted with a grace and a goodwill and a desire for peace which is, to my knowledge, unparalleled. Whether or not it was wise in the long term to do so, is another matter entirely.

The inauguration of the President was, however, something entirely different. Power was now changing hands in a visible way. Everyone stood with tears in our eyes and hope in our heart. These are some of Michael's impressions of those amazing days:

> I went to the Grand Parade, outside the Town Hall in Cape Town. Along with more than 100,000 others, we enjoyed a concert while awaiting the arrival of Nelson Mandela. Late in the morning, Mandela was elected by parliament as President of the Republic. Difficult to believe after more then 300 years, we had our first black President and the first democratically elected President. The mood of the people was one of bubbling over with joy. In the crowd I met old friends and those who have read articles I have written or seen TV interviews. One woman said she had just seen, over the weekend, a video which was made about my bombing. Eventually, the new leaders appeared on the balcony. Everyone cheered Thabo Mbeki, the First Deputy President. De Klerk was greeted with a mixture of cheers and boos. Everyone listened in rapt attention as Mandela spoke, simply and powerfully about the journey from 1652 to this day.
>
> I flew to Johannesburg on the Monday night. I stayed with friends who are part of ANC military health. On Tuesday April 10, we woke very early to be in Pretoria by 7:00 a.m.

The Pretoria streets were lined with soldiers from all the different military formations, including the People's Army, *Umkhonto We Sizwe.* The attitude of every person we met, many of whom were former enemies, whose job it was to kill us, was quite wonderful. It was difficult to believe that this day of days was actually happening. Even now, I half expect to wake up and find that it was all just a wonderful dream and that now I have woken up.

It was very appropriate that the inauguration took place at the Union Buildings — the center of *their* administrative power which was now becoming ours — all of us. I had many wonderful personal encounters at the inauguration. One woman said I had come to her house in 1973. A man reminded me that we had met at an ANC summer school in 1980. I met a mother whom I had supported when her son went to prison for seven and a half years. Beyers Naude, the Dutch Reformed Minister who joined the struggle, embraced me and with tears, thanked me for what I had done. I hugged Limpo Hani, Chris Hani's widow, whom I had not spoken to since the assassination of her husband. Joe Modise, commander of *Umkhonto We Sizwe,* said he had to hug me today. Alec Borraine, a former white opposition MP [now co-chair of the Truth and Reconciliation Commission, together with Desmond Tutu] said it was the first time he had felt proud to be a South African. I met Robert and Paula McBride. Robert is a freedom fighter who spent several years in Pretoria Central Prison on Death Row. For years, we had fought to save his life. When I was bombed, he had sent a message from the death cells.

Eventually, after having kept the world waiting for an hour, after the arrival of heads of state from everywhere, President Nelson Mandela arrived, preceded by all the heads of the armed forces, signalling that power is actually changing hands. After the Deputy Presidents, Nelson Mandela took the oath of office and the whole world cheered. He told us all: "Never, never and never again shall it be that this beautiful land will again experience the oppression of one by another. Let freedom reign. God bless Africa."

The 21 gun salute began. Then in the distance we saw the planes approaching — first helicopters and finally jet fighter with jet streams in the new national colors. For a moment the thought that they could bomb us, and the dawning realization that now for the first time, it was our air force, saluting our President...

It is a measure of the stature of the man, that now, when President Mandela addresses parliament, he is applauded by friend and foe alike. So deeply is he respected, so much is he admired. However, his presence in parliament is not enough to heal the nation. As a symbol he is extraordinarily important, but the nation needs to go beyond symbols and to contemplate and deal with reality. Michael understood this immediately: "Our ability to reconcile and create a new society is inextricably tied up with our ability to come to terms with the past."[16]

For the Nationalist Party, the party of apartheid, the cry has been that we should forget the past. Indeed, Michael refers to an incident when he and Professor Kader Asmal (now Minister of Water Affairs in the Government of National Unity), speaking on a radio program, made the obvious comparison between apartheid and nazism. Sheila Camerer, a Nationalist MP who was also on the program objected, that the remark was "in bad taste." In so doing, Michael retorted, she reduced the issue of the suffering caused by her party's policies down the years "to the level of whether someone uses bad language, or forgets to use a table napkin." [17] The truth needs to be told and to be heard. Without that, healing cannot take place, he continued. "Let the truth be told, all of it. Without the whole truth, healing will never come for the oppressed or the oppressors. We cannot forgive and forget what they have not yet been willing to remember."[18]

Significant sections of the South African population were "deaf and blind" to what was happening around them as well as to the "root causes" of it, "even when the whole world tried to tell them." In South Africa particularly, we have, what Michael calls a "divided memory."[19] Part of the process of "remembering" would be to integrate the national memory.

Michael often returns to a profound theological theme. The theme of anamnesis — "remembering."

---

[16] Michael Lapsley, letter to Gillian Hawney, April 18, 1995.

[17] Michael Lapsley, speech to the meeting to oppose the Further Indemnity Bill.

[18] Ibid.

[19] Michael Lapsley, interview for BBC Radio, April 13, 1995.

For Christians, we need to remind ourselves that we belong to a remembering religion. "Remember when you were slaves in Egypt" is the constant refrain of the Old Testament. The words of Jesus: "Do this in memory of me" are said at every Eucharist. The question is not one of forgetting but rather it is the problem of how do we deal with our memories. How do we stop our memories from destroying us?

Forgiveness, yes. That is always the Christian calling. But no one should suggest that forgiveness is glib, cheap or easy. What does it mean to forgive those who have not confessed; those who have not changed their lives; those who have no interest in making it up to the relatives of victims and the survivors of their crimes. If you forgive a murderer, it does not mean that there should be no justice. How do we achieve reconciliation as a nation? Can we forgive each other for what we have done?[20]

It was an old friend of Michael's, Horst Kleinschmidt, who when Michael lay in his hospital bed in Australia, telephoned and told him of the seeds of a project which was just starting in Cape Town. The idea was to set up a Trauma Center for victims of violence and torture in Cowley House. Appropriately, Cowley House was situated in that famous area of Cape Town called District Six, where people had been forcibly removed by the apartheid government because they were too dark or too mixed. In the end they were removed because District Six was a palpable sign that people of different colors could live together — could even want to live together! It was too much for the apartheid ideologists to bear. Thus District Six remained a festering sore in the life of the city. Cowley House, then, is a place pregnant with memories, because, for a number of years, it had been a halfway house for people visiting their relatives on Robben Island, apartheid's maximum security prison for its opponents. When Robben Island emptied as a political prison in 1990, the house became a kind of reception center. Health workers who had worked with detainees and political prisoners began to ask what should become of Cowley House. How could the emotional, psychological and spiritual wounds of the past begin to be addressed. Horst felt that Michael would be ideally qualified to work in such a center. Michael recalls this incident:

---

[20] Ibid.

What was wonderful to me was that people were busy telling me what I would not now be able to do, because I had no hands, because I had a major permanent disability. And here was someone who was saying, "You are going to be more qualified to do this than other people."[21]

Michael's appointment to the position of Chaplain to the Trauma Center was, he felt, "one of those things that was supposed to be."[22] His appointment was strongly backed by Archbishop Tutu and the other bishops of the Archdiocese as well as then Dean of Cape Town, Colin Jones, who all felt that this was something peculiarly appropriate for Michael, especially because the Trauma Center was to be a project of the South African Health and Social Services in partnership with the Anglican Church, which owned the building.

Upon taking up the post, it became very clear to Michael that he would not be able to deal with the pain and suffering of others if he had not begun to deal with his own:

If I were not at all facing what had happened to me, I could be more of a hindrance than a help in this kind of work. Insofar as I have been able to overcome and not been a prisoner of what has happened to me, so I think I am of some use, being trained as a priest and yet also having suffered pain and loss. I have a peculiar, special kind of role. My other colleagues with whom I work... have their own stories of pain and suffering and sacrifice to suit them as well for this type of work. Although they may not have the physical evidence of having lost hands [they have nonetheless]... other kinds of inner pain. Perhaps more importantly than what I show visibly, is the inner story of pain and suffering which is true of so many of our people.[23]

Michael is fond of saying that the stories of the victims must be "reverenced, acknowledged and recognized," and this as a process of "healing the memories" has become a major part of his work, since joining the Trauma Center staff.

---

[21] Michael Lapsley, interview with John Orr on the "Insights" program of Radio South Africa, May 22, 1994.

[22] Ibid.

[23] Ibid.

In many ways the kind of work I do now, in the Trauma Center is [with]... individuals seeking to heal their memories. And part of that healing process, a very important part, is that there has to be full disclosure. The truth has to be told and that is an extremely important step for the process of healing to take place...[24]

The Truth and Reconciliation Commission is in complete accord with this sentiment. There cannot be reconciliation if there has not been truth. The truth must be told. It must be heard. No matter what and how and who and where. If there is to be reconciliation, if there is to be forgiveness, if there is to be healing and wholeness in this wounded land, there must be full disclosure.

The [Truth and Reconciliation] Commission turns its back on any desire for revenge. It represents an extraordinary act of generosity by a people who only insist that the truth, the whole truth and nothing but the truth must be told. The space is thereby created where the deeper processes of forgiveness, confession, repentance, reparation and reconciliation can take place.[25]

— oOo —

---

[24] Ibid.

[25] Michael Lapsley, letter to Gillian Hawney, April 18, 1995.

Postscript

The story that I have told has many players. Some of them are heroic, some of them are less, few are bad. The tragedy of the years of apartheid was that they called for heroes — not just one or two, but thousands, millions. Most people are not heroic. This does not make them bad. With hindsight, many if not most of us, might well have acted differently in this drama. Different decisions might well have been made. Less hurts might well have been caused. Less pain, maybe. Maybe even less bombs might have been made and less shots fired.

But what is true about this story is that all the actors — from the bomber to Michael, from the archbishop to the altar-server, from the Jack to the Queen — share one thing in common. They are all human. We share this humanity with each other in life and in death, in sickness and in health. Can Michael forgive the bomber? That is his decision — but the truth must first be heard. Can we South Africans forgive each other? Yes, but we need to hear the truth before we can be reconciled, at the very least. We need to hear. We need to weep. We need to listen and weep again. And then — we need to forgive each other; and recognize each other and learn to live together in peace and build a future where everyone can feel secure and at home. This has become a constant theme for Michael:

> I find that with many of the people I work with, part of the problem is that what has been done to them has not been publicly recognized and acknowledged by those who did it and by the wider society. And I think that is important, if we are going to break the cycle of bitterness, hatred and revenge. I think there is a willingness in the nation to do this, but the temptation is that we will bury the memories rather than heal them. If we do that, it will burst out in various destructive ways in the life of the nation for many, many years to come.[26]

Michael underwent a slight (perhaps a major) personality change after the bombing. Many people have noticed this, and he has even

---

[26] Ibid.

noticed it himself. The bombing made Michael a much gentler person than he was before. He has come to value people, to honor people in a way in which he never did before. Do not misunderstand — Michael is no saint, or if he is, so are we all. We are all disabled in one way or another. When he has preached on the theme of forgiveness, he has often ended his sermon in this way:

> I stand before you in a small way, as a sign of what apartheid has done. Of the physical brokenness that it has caused. We are all, in a sense, disabled people. But I think I stand before you in a more important way, as a sign of the power of God. A sign that there is something stronger. Something stronger than the evil and the hatred and the death that apartheid embodies and represents. And that is the power of God. I stand before you in a small way as the sign of the power of love, of gentleness and compassion. The power of life is stronger than hatred and death and in the power of God — we will win. Amen.[27]

May we all, in this life we live together, seek in a small and even a big way, to be a sign of the power of love, of gentleness and compassion. May we learn together how to forgive and to heal the memories and the many wounds.

---

[27] Michael Lapsley, sermon, "South Africa, the end and the beginning are near," preached at the Canaan Baptist Church of Christ on 116th Street, Harlem, New York, December 5, 1993.

LIST OF ABBREVIATIONS:

ANC	African National Congress
ANSOCS	Anglican Societies (student)
ASF	Anglican Students' Federation
AZAPO	Azanian People's Organization
BNP	Basotholand National Party
CCB	Civil Cooperation Bureau
CPSA	Church of the Province of Southern Africa
CR	Community of the Resurrection
LIC	Low intensity conflict
MK	Umkhonto We Sizwe (Spear of the Nation)
MNR	Mozambique National Resistance
PAC	Pan Africanist Congress (of Azania)
PCR	Program to Combat Racism
PLO	Palestine Liberation Organization
RENAMO	National Resistance Movement of Mozambique
RSA	Republic of South Africa
SACP	South African Communist Party
SADF	South African Defense Force
SASOL	South African Steel, Oil and Gas Corporation
SB	Special Branch of the South African Police Force
SSM	Society of the Sacred Mission
SWAPO	South West African People's Organization
UDF	United Democratic Front
UDI	Unilateral Declaration of Independence (Zimbabwe)
UNITA	National Union for the Total Independence of Angola
WCC	World Council of Churches

INDEX

Also published by Ocean Press

CHANGING THE HISTORY OF AFRICA
Angola and Namibia
by Gabriel García Márquez, Jorge Risquet, Fidel Castro
ISBN 1-875284-00-1   200 pages, photos

FIDEL AND RELIGION
Conversations with Frei Betto
ISBN 1-875284-05-2   268 pages, photos

I WAS NEVER ALONE
A prison diary from El Salvador
by Nidia Díaz
ISBN 1-875284-13-3   210 pages, photos

SLOVO
The unfinished autobiography of ANC leader Joe Slovo
ISBN 1-875284-95-8   250 pages, photos

AFROCUBA
An anthology of Cuban writing on race, politics and culture
Edited by Pedro Pérez Sarduy and Jean Stubbs
ISBN 1-875284-41-9   309 pages

CHE
A memoir by Fidel Castro
Edited by David Deutschmann
ISBN 1-875284-15-X   165 pages, photos

For a list of Ocean Press distributors, see copyright page
◆